Galileo

Galileo :
the Scientific Revolution

Edward Singleton Holden

Man and Society Studies Collection

LM Publishers

Chapter I

When the position of a heavenly body changes with such extreme slowness as to leave astronomers undecided as to the change even, and still more as to the direction of the change, it is their custom to compare two observations made at a great interval of time. If the doubt still exists, they affirm with certainty that the position they have measured is invariable, or nearly so, since it is subject to no regular and persistent alteration. Such a method applied to the history of the human mind leads to grave melancholy and discouragement. Men have been ignorant and blind at every epoch. Always we find the same ignorance, the same rash illusions, the same obstinate prejudices.

Three centuries before our era, a philosopher, Cleanthes, demanded that Aristarchus should be brought to justice for his blasphemies in declaring the earth in motion, and the sun to be the fixed centre of the universe. Two thousand years later, the human understanding had not progressed. The desire of Cleanthes was realized, and Galileo was accused of blasphemy and impiety, in his turn. A tribunal dreaded by all condemned his writings, constrained him to denials disavowed by his conscience, and, judging him unworthy of a freedom that he had abused, deprived him of a part of it, and thought it an indulgence to have left him any liberty whatever.

But history is not to be judged in this way. Events in themselves are of small moment; the impression that events produce is the only revelation of the public consciousness. Never before has its generous aversion for intolerance burst forth so strongly as for the sufferings of Galileo. The story of his misfortunes, exaggerated like a pious legend, has confirmed the triumph of the truths for which he suffered, at the same time avenging him. The scandal of his condemnation will forever vex the pride of those who still wish to put down reason by force; and the just severity of opinion will preserve the unwelcome remembrance as an eternal reproach. But it is necessary to be frank: this great lesson did not cause any deep sorrows. The long life of Galileo, taken all in all, is one of the most peaceful and most enviable that the history of science records.

The foregoing paragraphs translated freely from the life of Galileo by M. Bertrand, perpetual secretary of the Paris Academy of Sciences, expresses so precisely the point of view of this article that I have quoted them in order to have, from the outset, the support of his great authority. And to them may be added the following extracts from the 'History of the Inductive Sciences' of Dr. Whewell, master of Trinity College, Cambridge. The words in brackets are my own.

The heliocentric doctrine has for a century been making its way into the minds of thoughtful men on the general ground of its simplicity and symmetry. Galileo appears to have thought that now, when these original recommendations of the system had been reenforced by his own discoveries and reasonings, it ought to be universally acknowledged as a truth and a reality. And when arguments against the fixity of the sun and the motion of the earth were adduced from scripture, he could not be satisfied without maintaining his favorite opinion to be conformable to scripture as well as to philosophy; and he was very eager in his attempts to obtain from authority a declaration to this effect. The ecclesiastical authorities were naturally averse to express themselves in favor of a novel opinion, startling to the common mind, and contrary to the most obvious meaning of the words of the Bible; and when they were compelled to pronounce, they decided against Galileo and his doctrines. He was accused before the Inquisition in 1615; . . . the result was a declaration of the Inquisition that the doctrine of the earth's motion [was] contrary to the sacred scripture. Galileo was prohibited from defending and teaching this doctrine in any manner, and promised obedience to this injunction [as will be shown later].

But in 1632 he published his Dialogues and in these he defended the heliocentric system by all the strongest arguments which its admirers used. Not only so, but he introduced into this dialogue a character under the name of Simplicius [supposed by contemporaries to have been intended to represent the Pope then reigning, which idea was fully accepted by the Pope himself, especially as the Pope's own words were attributed to Simplicius,] in whose mouth was put the defense of all the ancient dogmas and who was represented as defeated at all points of the discussion; and he prefixed to the dialogue a notice To the Discreet Reader, in which, in a view of transparent irony he assigned his reasons for the publication. . . . The result of this was that Galileo was condemned for his infraction of the injunction laid upon him in 1616; his dialogue was prohibited; he himself was commanded to abjure on his knees the doctrine he had taught; and this abjuration he performed.

. . . The general acceptance of the Copernican system was no longer a matter of doubt. Several persons in the highest positions including the Pope himself [not the Pope] looked upon the doctrine with favorable eyes; and had shown their interest in Galileo and his discoveries. They had tried to prevent his involving himself in trouble by [through] discussing the question on scriptural grounds. It is probable that his knowledge of those favorable dispositions towards himself and his opinions led him to suppose that the slightest color of professed submission to the church in his belief, would enable his arguments in favor of the system to pass unvisited; the notice [To the Discreet Reader] in which the irony is quite transparent and the sarcasm glaringly obvious, was deemed too flimsy a veil for the purpose of decency, and, indeed, must have aggravated the offence.

The foregoing extracts from the writings of authoritative historians of science place the chief events of Galileo's long life in what seems to be the true light. There is little doubt as to the events themselves—except in a single particular, which will be considered in what follows. Much controversy has raged over their interpretation. They must be considered in two regards: First, in respect of Galileo's private and personal experience; second, in respect of the lesson which that experience has taught to the world in general. The remark of Bertrand that has just been quoted is profoundly significant: *events in themselves are small affairs; it is their effect on the public consciousness that remains and is permanent.* Galileo's private life was essentially peaceful, as a whole even 'enviable.' To the world in general he is, on the other hand, the protomartyr. His trials have opened new roads for human thought, given liberty to science and philosophy, and were the occasion of a final delimitation of the provinces of the church and of philosophy. The modern attitude of mind may be said to take its date from him. It is in this that his greatest service to mankind consists. The astonishing discoveries that we owe to his genius are small matters in comparison.

In what follows the events of his life will be recited. Where there is doubt it will be pointed out. There is no space to discuss controverted points at length. Volumes have already been written on the history of his trial by the Inquisition; on the documents, genuine or fabricated, of this process; on the question whether or no he was put to the torture. To these volumes reference must be made, once for all, for the original documents and for a discussion of their authenticity. The object of the present chapter is, first, to tell the story of his life, second, and most important, to exhibit its effect upon his own and succeeding centuries. It will conduce to clearness if his private and personal life be separated in thought from his services to mankind in general; if the story of his experience be discriminated from the legend.

The popular legend in its crudest form declared that Galileo, a martyr of science, languished in the dungeons of the Inquisition; defended his doctrines boldly; was tortured; and under bodily torture recanted and abjured; saying, however, at the last, *E pur si muove* before he was again removed to his prison, where his eyes were blinded. If the legend had not taken on this crude shape it would, perhaps, have been less efficacious in the century immediately following his death. As it stands it is almost entirely devoid of truth. The real history is hardly less distressing, but the facts are utterly different.

Galileo was born at Pisa on February 18, 1564, of the noble family of the Bonajuti which since

1343 had been known as the Galilei. In 1445 a representative of the family was Gonfalonier of Florence, and no less than fifteen of its members had served in the Signoria. The father of Galileo, Vincenzio, was skilled in mathematics and especially in music, on which he wrote several treatises. He was poor and wished his brilliant son to adopt the lucrative profession of medicine. Galileo's early inclinations seem to have been to become a painter. The boy was educated at the monastery of Vallombrosa, where he learned Latin, some Greek, a little logic. He was an excellent pupil, but as his eyes were affected his father removed him and, at the age of seventeen (1581), sent him to study medicine at Pisa. He was already a clever musician, witty, eloquent, with a strong talent for painting, and had laid the foundations of a literary style which Italians estimate highly. In his later years Galileo knew the poems of Ariosto by heart. His general health was not good, but he was amiable, gay, versatile, fond of society and also very fond of a country life and of his vineyards and groves. He was considerate and liberal to his family, devoted to his children. His friends loved him ardently, and his enemies were equally constant in their dislike. The characteristics of his maturer life were in evidence throughout his youth also. His powers of observation were extraordinarily quick. He was a philosopher, also, from the first, and very expert in all mechanical matters.

Before the high altar of the cathedral at Pisa hangs a lamp,—a masterpiece of Maestro Possenti. Watching its swingings to and fro one day Galileo, then a student, observed that although the amplitude of the swings diminished the time of oscillation remained the same (1583). From this chance observation resulted the law: The time of oscillation of a pendulum is independent of the amplitude of its swings. If this be true (and it is true when the amplitudes are small), the pendulum can be used to measure, with precision, intervals of time. A hundred of its swings will always require the same time whenever the arc of swinging is not large. The first application of this discovery was the invention of a pendulum suited to measure pulse-beats. Towards the end of his life Galileo endeavored to construct a pendulum clock. He was engaged in this research at the time of his death, aided by his son Vincenzio, who carried on the work. A short pendulum beats more quickly than a long one. The law of the relation of length to period was also discovered by Galileo. It is: The lengths of pendulums are proportional to the squares of the times of oscillation. A pendulum beating seconds is four times as long as one beating half-seconds, therefore. These laws are the basis of horology. They were first fully utilized in the construction of clocks by Huyghens.

A lesson in geometry overheard by Galileo while a pupil excited his deepest interest. Euclid soon became his master and, from this day, his attention to medicine slackened, much to his father's regret. The salaries of mathematical professors were extremely small in those days, while the rewards of successful physicians were very much greater. Owing to his father's poverty, Galileo was withdrawn from the university in 1586, and returned to Florence. It is recorded that at the university he was known as a brilliant, though disputatious, pupil, and was nicknamed 'The Wrangler.' At Florence he lectured before the academy on the situation and dimensions of the Inferno of Dante—a question partly philosophical, partly scientific. It was at this time that he studied the works of Archimedes and wrote a little treatise on the hydrostatic balance. In 1587 he went to Rome and made the acquaintance of Clavius and other scientific men.

In 1588 he had the great good fortune to meet a generous patron, the Marchese Guidobaldo del Monte, and, in the same year, wrote at his request a treatise on the center of gravity of solid bodies. By his influence Galileo was appointed to be lecturer on mathematics in the University of Pisa (1589). His salary was only sixty scudi annually (about $65), and he was obliged to eke it out by giving private lessons. The salary of the professor of medicine was 2,000 scudi. During the years 1589 to 1591 he made those experiments on falling bodies which are the basis of the science of mechanics.

From the time of Archimedes (287-212 B.C.) till that of Leonardo da Vinci and Galileo there had been no progress in theoretical mechanics. Archimedes discovered the theory of the lever: 'Give me where I may stand and (with the lever) I will move the world.' His knowledge of practical mechanics was, no doubt, derived from his famous works of military engineering. All the great buildings of antiquity had been built by processes not unfamiliar to him. All the great basilicas of Europe and all the Gothic cathedrals with their nice system of balanced thrusts had also been erected before the time of Leonardo. The practical processes of engineering were highly developed, therefore, but as yet no one had formulated a theory. That Leonardo comprehended its fundamentals is abundantly shown by his note-books recently published. Every military engineer who had watched the flight of a projectile was aware that the received notions of mechanics would not explain its motions. No theory of the impact of such projectiles had even been proposed. A whole science was to be created. The doctrine of mechanical equilibrium is statics—and this science was founded by Archimedes. The doctrine of mechanical motion is dynamics—and nothing was done in this science till the time of Galileo. The theories of the lever, of the inclined plane and of the screw were familiar to Leonardo.

The ideas of Aristotle as to motion and rest were not physical, hut metaphysical. An example will illustrate his mode of reasoning which satisfied the scientific world for something like two thousand years. When a stone is thrown from the hand why does it continue to move for a time, and why does it eventually come to rest? Where is the cause of motion—in the hand?—or in the stone? If in the hand, how can the stone continue to move after it has left the hand? If in the stone, why does it ever come to rest? Aristotle's answer is that 'a motion is communicated to the air, the successive parts of which urge the stone onward; each portion of the air continues to act for some little time after it has been acted upon, and the motion ceases when it comes to a particle which cannot act after it has been acted upon.' The confusion of this explanation is complete.

The mechanical ideas of Aristotle and of his successors, as to falling bodies, are expressed in these words: 'That body, is heavier than another which, in an equal bulk, moves downward quicker.' Transforming the phrase, we may say, that if two bodies, A and B, are of equal bulk but of different weights, then the heavier body will fall the quicker; or, again, if A weighs ten pounds and B one pound, A will fall faster than B. The Aristotelians of Galileo's time further maintained that A would fall exactly ten times faster than B. Galileo's experiments proved that they fell in precisely the same time. Sixteen hundred years earlier Lucretius had come near to the same truth: "For whenever bodies fall through water and thin air they must quicken their descents in proportion to their weights, because the body of water and subtle nature of air cannot retard everything to an equal degree; on the other hand, empty void cannot offer resistance to anything in any direction at any time, but must continually give way; and for this reason all things must be moved and borne along with equal velocity, though of unequal weights, through the unresisting void."

While Kepler was determining the empirical laws according to which the planets move in their orbits, Galileo was laying the foundations of the science of mechanics by which, eventually, Newton was to explain why they so move. The foundations of mechanics rest on experiments made by Galileo, at Pisa, on the laws of falling bodies. It was the opinion of the time that heavy bodies fell faster than light ones, and it was a matter of common observation that a square foot of wood reached the ground before a square foot of paper released at the same time. The fact was explained by Galileo as due to the resistance of the air. In a vacuum they would fall at the same time. By crumpling the paper into a solid ball, it could be made to fall as rapidly as a ball of wood or iron. Experiments of this nature led Galileo to the discovery of the first law of motion, to wit: The velocity of falling bodies varies directly as the time.

At the beginning of the fall the velocity is zero; at the end of the first second, it is a certain quantity which experiment shows to be the same for all bodies. Let us call this velocity g. Galileo's experiments showed that at the end of the second second the terminal velocity was $2g$, at the end of the third, $3g$ and so on. The algebraic expression of the first law is, then,

(I.) $v = g.t$

(experiment shows that # = 9.81 meters approximately).

The second law of motion refers to the relation of the spaces through which the body falls in different intervals of time; it is: The spaces through which a body falls vary as the squares of the times. All bodies obey this law, also, no matter of what materials they are made up.

(II.) $s = \frac{1}{2}g.t^2$
(s = space, t = time).

At the beginning of the fall the time (t) is zero, and the velocity (v) is also zero. At the end of the first second, $t = 1$ and $v = g$ (by I.). The velocity has increased from 0 to g and its average value is therefore $0+g/2 = \frac{1}{2}g$. The space traversed at the end of the first second is (by II.) $\frac{1}{2}g$; at the end of the second second, $2g$; at the end of the third second, and so on. The two laws are not independent but are separated for convenience. They are sometimes united into one, and the law of inertia (also known to Galileo) added in this form: Everybody preserves its state of rest or of uniform motion in a right line unless it is compelled to change that state by forces impressed thereon.

It is this latter law that changed the whole face of science. It was supposed by the ancients and by Copernicus that the normal condition of all bodies was rest; that if they were moving it was because some force was perpetually impelling them. On the earth a pendulum stops because of the resistance of the air and the friction at its supports. Remove the air and annul the friction and it will swing forever until some impressed force stops it, so Galileo announced. Kepler was incessantly trying to conceive how a planet could continue to move in its orbit, and was forced to conclude that some inherent energy, perhaps an angel, perpetually acted to keep it moving. Galileo's law announces that if it is once set in motion it will continue to move until some impressed and extraneous force causes it to stop. Motion is as 'natural' as rest, therefore. It happens that on the earth there is no body moving under the action of no force. Falling bodies, projectiles, and the like, are perpetually attracted by the earth's mass, continually retarded by the resistance of the air. It required abstract philosophical reasoning to determine how such bodies would move were the impressed forces removed, and it is this reasoning that is Galileo's chief title to enduring fame. In this respect he changed the whole thought of the world. His telescopic discoveries might have been made by others. There was no man in Italy besides himself who could have founded the new science of mechanics.

Newton added two laws of motion which read: The alternation of motion is ever proportional to the moving force impressed and is made in the right line in which that force acts. To every action there is always opposed an equal reaction; or the mutual actions of two bodies upon each other are always equal, and in opposite directions. His law of universal gravitation is: Every particle of matter in the universe attracts every other particle with a force directly as the masses of the two particles, and inversely as the squares of the distance that separates them.

With these laws as bases of calculation the question may be answered: What orbit will a planet describe about the sun? The answer is, a conic section, an ellipse for example. Again: What will be the law of the motion of each planet in its ellipse? The answer is: Its radius-vector will sweep over equal areas in equal times. Again: In a system of such planets, how will their orbits be related? The answer is: The squares of their periodic times will be proportional to the cubes of their mean distances from the sun. From the single law of gravitation the three laws of Kepler (as above) necessarily follow. Kepler's laws were empirical and were not complete until Newton's discoveries. This brief note explains the logical outcome of Kepler's and of Galileo's researches.

The new laws of motion were expounded to the students of Pisa with fire and eloquence. The theories of Aristotle and of his followers were treated with scorn and contempt. In his zeal for the truth Galileo branded the scientific errors of his colleagues almost as if they had been moral faults. His asperity laid the foundation of enmities that followed him throughout the whole of his life and led to his ruin. It is as true of Galileo as of Roger Bacon that his character was his fate.

How the strictures of Galileo were received by the exasperated Aristotelians may be imagined. If his experiments were to be believed, the words of Aristotle were false. If the philosophy of Aristotle were false in one part it might be false in all. The experiments must therefore be denied, and their author discredited. It is recorded that the experiments were, in fact, denied. The facts of experience were met with argument. Galileo's retorts were bitter and brilliant, his sarcasms searching and unsparing. Before the end of his three years' engagement as professor had expired, he had involved himself in a hopeless wrangle with his colleagues and with Aristotelians throughout Italy. An imbroglio with John of Medici put him out of favor at court also at this very time. The nephew of the reigning Duke of Florence had invented a machine for dredging the harbor of Leghorn, and the plans were submitted to Galileo, who declared the apparatus to be useless, as indeed it was. He made no friends by this candor and gave another weapon to his enemies which they were not slow to use. The students in the university were incited against him and he was publicly hissed at lectures, so that he felt it advisable to resign his professorship (1591).

He returned to Florence discredited and out of favor. His father died in July of this year, leaving his family in distress for money. Galileo's friend and patron, the Marquis del Monte, warmly recommended him to his friends in Venice, and as a result he was appointed to be professor of mathematics at the University of Padua, for a term of six years, this time at a salary of 72 zecchini, about $90. He remained titular professor for a period of eighteen years, until 1610, his appointment being three times renewed and his emoluments increased to $500. In December, 1592, he entered upon his duties. His lessons embraced a wide range of subjects: astronomy, gnomonics, fortification, mechanics and the like. His lectures were thronged with students. The halls were not spacious enough to hold them all and at times he taught in the open air.

In 1597 he invented his proportional compasses of which he was very proud. His manuscript description of them was plagiarized by one Balthasar Capra, and Galileo's scathing review of the work excited general notice for its bitter satire. He was already recognized as an adversary to be feared.

It has lately been demonstrated that we owe the invention of the thermometer to Galileo. His first instrument appears to have been a crude air thermometer devised in 1595. It was soon (1611) applied by physicians to the diagnosis of fevers and about 1641 to regular meteorological observations of temperature. The scales were arbitrary. The idea was developed by his pupils in various ways. The 'Florentine' thermometers used by the Accademia del Cimento (1657-1667) had straight sealed tubes connected with bulbs filled with spirits of wine. The highest summer heat corresponded to 80°, the lowest winter cold to 20°. So late as 1741 Florentine thermometers were in common use throughout Europe. It was not till 1694 that the freezing and boiling points of water were *proposed* as standard. Fahrenheit's thermometer date from 1709, Réaumer's from 1730, Celsius's (the centigrade) from 1742-3.

In 1604 a new star suddenly appeared in the heavens. It was discovered in October and quickly grew to be brighter than Jupiter. By the end of March, 1605, it had diminished to the brightness of a star of the third magnitude and in about a year it had vanished from sight. Its career was like that of the new star of 1572— Tycho's star. Galileo delivered three lectures on the new star to crowded audiences. He enforced upon the Aristotelians the conclusion that the heavens were not incorruptible, as they maintained. Here was a glaring proof of it. The star had no parallax. Hence it was far beyond our atmosphere. It was no 'meteor,' as they also maintained. These just conclusions were advanced with rasping criticisms of the old philosophy and the breach with his colleagues was widened still further.

In 1597 Kepler sent his *Prodromus* to Galileo, who writes to thank him for it, saying:

> I count myself happy, in the search after truth, to have so great an ally as yourself. . . . I have been for many years an adherent of the Copernican system. . . . I have collected many arguments for the purpose of refuting (the commonly accepted hypothesis), but I do not venture to the light of publicity for fear of sharing the fate of our master Copernicus, who, although he has earned immortal fame with some, yet with very many— so great is the number of fools—has become an object of ridicule and scorn.

It is to be noticed that Galileo (like Copernicus himself) dreaded the ridicule of fools. It is probable that neither of them feared the discipline of the church, or even considered it likely to be exerted.

The revolution in men's ideas to be worked by the Copernican system was not understood in the sixteenth century. It was regarded as a scientific hypothesis—an absurd one, contrary to scripture, Tycho Brahe had said. Its theological import was appreciated first by Lutherans and afterwards in Italy. Pope Paul III., to whom Copernicus dedicated his book in 1543, received it 'with pleasure.' A second edition was printed in 1566 without exciting the slightest adverse remark. It was not until the time of Galileo that men began to see that the accepted order of heaven and earth was inverted by the new doctrine. The earth was no longer the center of the universe. The planets were not made for man, who was dethroned not only in science, but in philosophy and theology as well. It remained for more modern times to appreciate that as it was by man himself that man was so dethroned, a new glory had been added to his crown.

All men find it painful to face novel ideas, and it is but natural to seek and find sufficient reasons for avoiding painful thoughts. When they are once familiar, new pleasures are discovered; and not until then do they begin to gain acceptance. Kepler 'shuddered' at the very idea of an infinite universe. Even he had not completely shaken off the Ptolemaic conception of a limited world. The authority of the Roman

Church had been in theory literally universal, and Copernicus limited its world to one small planet, not so large as Jupiter as Galileo showed a few years later. The new doctrine disgraced the dignity of the earth among the planets. The authorities of a universal church could not but feel that their own dignities were attacked by the same blow. Arguments against the scientific truth were forthcoming from every chair of philosophy in Italy, and every theologian could successfully defend the literal sense of Holy Writ against such subtle and wire-drawn interpretations as were subsequently advanced by Foscarini and Galileo. I imagine the state of mind of their more intelligent contemporaries to have been one of interested bewilderment. The less intelligent were repelled and offended. The mass of pious christians was outraged and indignant. The Pope (Urban VIII.) and most of the cardinals sincerely believed that incalculable injury would result to the church from the promulgation of an opinion flatly contradicting the literal words of scripture. It was not until the discoveries of the telescope came to confirm the hypothesis of Copernicus that all these questions were pressed home for decision.

Chapter II

Galileo in the *Sidereus Nuncius* (1610) gives this account of the invention of the telescope:

> A report reached my ears that a Dutchman had constructed a telescope, by the aid of which visible objects, although at a great distance from the observer, were seen distinctly as if near.... A few days after, I received confirmation of the report in a letter... which finally determined me to inquire into the principle of the telescope and then to consider the means by which I might compass the invention of a similar instrument, which, in a little while, I succeeded in doing, through deep study of the theory of refraction.... At length I succeeded in constructing for myself an instrument so superior that objects seen through it appeared... more than thirty times nearer than if viewed by the natural powers of sight alone.

On the title page of his book the telescope is described as 'lately invented by him.' This claim Galileo does not make, but in subsequent years it was charged by his enemies that he claimed credit not his due, and the charge perpetually reappears. The amazing discoveries of this memorable year are enumerated on the title page in question.

The Sidereal Messinger (Nuncius Sidereus), unfolding great and very wonderful spectacles and offering them to the consideration of everyone, especially of philosophers and astronomers; being such as have been observed by Galileo Galilei... by the assistance of a perspective glass lately invented by him; namely, in the face of the Moon, an innumerable number of fixed stars, the Milky Way, and nebulous stars, but especially respecting four Planets that revolve about Jupiter at different intervals and periods with a wonderful celerity; which, hitherto not known to any one, the author has recently been the first to discover and has decreed to call the Medicean Stars. (Venice, 1610.)

The surface of the moon was covered with brilliant and dark areas as the peacock's tail with spots. Perhaps the moon has an atmosphere, he says. The heights of lunar mountains can be fixed by measuring their shadows. The ashy-light of the moon ('old moon in the new moon's arms') is perhaps caused by a lunar twilight. He gives Leonardo da Vinci's explanation also—the true one—that it is caused by earth-light reflected to the moon and back to us. The stars appear as points of light, the planets as small discs. The telescope brings countless new stars to light. In the belt and sword of Orion he sees eighty stars where only seven were known before; in the Pleiades forty instead of six or seven. The Milky Way is a multitude of faint stars clustered together. The nebulas of Orion and Praesepe are formed of stars. His discovery of the moons of Jupiter dates from January 7, 1610, when three of them were seen. They describe circular orbits about their planet. Jupiter, like each of the planets, has an atmosphere, he says. His telescope was not perfect enough to show this. It is a deduction from analogy.

New discoveries soon followed in respect to Saturn (Dec., 1610) and Venus (Jan., 1611), and they were announced in anagrams as follows:

SMAISMRMILMEPOETALEVMIBVNENVGTTAVIRAS.
ALTISSIMVM PLANETAM TERGEMINVM OBSERVAVI.
(*I have observed the highest planet—Saturn—to be triform.*)
HÆC IMMATURA À ME JAM FEUSTRA LEGUNTUR, O. Y.
CYNTHIA FIGURAS AEMULATUR MATER AMORUM.
(*The mother of the loves—Venus—emulates the figure of Cynthia—the Moon.*)

The latter discovery was of capital importance. If the planet Venus revolved about the sun as Copernicus had said, it must show phases like the moon. The phases, invisible to Copernicus, were revealed by the telescope. They occurred at the precise times required to demonstrate the truth of his theory. It was now no longer a theory. It was proved. From this moment no competent witness could doubt the truth of the Copernican system—Galileo less than anyone.

An opportunity unique in the history of the world was presented to Galileo and he utilized it to the full. He went from triumph to triumph. The phases of Venus, the mountains of the moon, the constitution of the Milky Way, the tricorporate figure of Saturn, the solar spots, the moons of Jupiter, were death-blows to the systems of Aristotle and of Ptolemy, and were skilfully utilized to establish the system of Copernicus. That system rests, for us, not on the telescopic discoveries of Galileo, but on the working out of its details by Kepler and Newton. To the Italians of Galileo's day Kepler was all but unknown; it is even doubtful whether Galileo appreciated Kepler's splendid discoveries; it is, at any rate, certain that he never publicly mentioned them with praise.

The mere fact that the number of planets and satellites was increased by Galileo's telescope from seven to eleven was another blow to ancient superstitions. Seven was a mystic and magical number. It had relations even to Christianity, so his contemporaries thought. The seven golden candlesticks of Revelations were the seven planets. We can form some idea of the hold of certain magical numbers on the imaginations of our ancestors by remembering that when Huyghens discovered a satellite to

Saturn—thus raising the number of celestial bodies to twelve—he looked no more, 'because twelve was universally admitted to be a perfect number.' There were six planets and six satellites and he ventured to predict that no more would be discovered. Huyghens died in the year 1695. He was the foremost man of science on the continent of Europe.

In 1610 Galileo had seen Saturn 'tricorporate'—in December, 1612, he writes:

> Looking on Saturn I found it solitary without the assistance of its accustomed stars and, in short, perfectly round and defined like Jupiter; and such it still remains. Now, what can be said of so strange a metamorphosis? Are the two smaller stars consumed like the spots on the Sun? Have they suddenly vanished and fled? or has Saturn devoured his own children? or was the appearance indeed fraud and illusion, with which the glasses have for so long time mocked me, and so many others who have so often observed with me? Now, perhaps, the time is come to revive the withering hopes of those who, guided by more profound contemplations, have followed all the fallacies of the new observations, and recognized their impossibilities. I cannot resolve what to say in a juncture so strange, so new and so unexpected. The shortness of the time, the unexampled occurrence, the weakness of my intellect, and the terror of being mistaken, have greatly confounded me.

The explanation of the disappearance of the ansæ of Saturn's ring was not given until 1656 (by Huyghens). Galileo's telescope was not sufficiently perfect and he died without solving what was a mere riddle to him.

The spots on the sun were first seen by Galileo, though they were first described by others (Fabritius, Schemer). In April, 1611, Galileo exhibited them at Rome to an audience of notabilities. His own observations had convinced him, he says, that the spots were real; that they were not fixed at one part of the solar globe; that they had motions; he sees no reason to doubt that they are attached to the surface of the sun; he believes that they form at the sun's surface, are dissipated and may reappear. By August, 1612, he made other observations which confirmed his earlier conjectures. Their motions prove that the sun is spherical and that it turns on an axis. He notes also that the spots all lie within certain special zones of latitude. He observes the sun by projection—by receiving its image on a sheet of cardboard. Certain large spots can be seen by the naked eye, but by an inveterate prejudice that the heavenly bodies are incorruptible, they have not been remarked; to the shame of astronomers, he says, such appearances have previously been taken for Mercury in transit over the solar disc.

Galileo's discoveries were received with incredulity by the wisest men of Italy. The warm-hearted Kepler (April, 1610) was the first to recognize 'the divinity of his genius.' Little by little they made their way as Galileo demonstrated them triumphantly to friends and enemies. Arguments of all sorts were brought against them and against the heliocentric theory which they supported.

Animals, which move, have limbs and muscles; the earth has no limbs and muscles, therefore it does not move. It is angels who make Saturn, Jupiter, the sun, etc., turn round. If the earth revolved, it must, also, have an angel in the center to set it in motion; but only devils live there; it would therefore be a devil who would impart motion to the earth. . . . (Scipio Chiaramonti.)

Since it can be certainly gathered from Scripture that the heavens move above the earth, and since a circular motion requires something fixed around which to move . . . the earth is at the center of the universe. (Polocco, 1644.)

If the earth is a planet, and only one among several planets, it cannot be that any such great things have been done especially for it as the Christian doctrine teaches. If there are other planets, since God makes nothing in vain, they must be inhabited; but how can their inhabitants be descended from Adam? How can they trace back their origin to Noah's ark? How can they have been redeemed by the Savior?

The last paragraph is probably an answer to Galileo's opinion (December, 1612) that the moon and planets may be inhabited, though by creatures different from ourselves. Galileo writes to Kepler (August, 1610):

> You are the first and almost the only person who . . . has given entire credence to my statements. . . . We will not trouble ourselves about the abuse of the multitude. . . . In Pisa, Florence, Bologna, Venice and Padua many have seen the planets; but all are silent on the subject and undecided. . . . What is to be done? . . . I think, my Kepler, we will laugh at the extraordinary stupidity of the multitude. What do you say to the leading philosophers of the faculty here, to whom I have offered a thousand times to show my studies, but who . . . have never consented to look at planets, nor Moon, nor telescope? Verily, just as serpents close their ears, so do these men close their eyes to the light of truth. . . . People of this sort think that philosophy is a kind of book like the Aeneid or the Odyssey and that the truth is to be sought, not in the universe, not in nature, but (I use their own words) by comparing texts! How you would laugh, he goes on, if you heard the first philosopher of Pisa trying to 'argue the new planets out of heaven.'

While Galileo was teaching the elements of Euclid at Padua his colleague, Cremonini, was expounding Aristotle's *de Cœlo*. It was Cremonini who refused to look at the newly discovered satellites of Jupiter through the telescope, alleging as a reason that their existence was quite contrary to Aristotle's philosophy. It was the same Cremonini who, in 1619, with a dignity and firmness that must be sincerely admired, flatly refused to change the substance of his university lectures at the demand of the Grand Inquisitor of Padua. His duty was to expound the words of Aristotle as he found them, he said; he declined to teach as Aristotle's any doctrine that he did not sincerely believe to be the master's. Let this manly stand be counted off against his refusal to be convinced against authority. He is reputed to have been the last scholastic. When he died, in 1631, there was no one to take his place. The times had changed. We are accustomed to attribute all the merit of the change to Galileo, whose career so brilliantly represents what was best in the new scientific spirit. It is impossible to declare what the movement of the world would have been had Galileo never lived. It would, perhaps, have been much the same. A company of less brilliant men would, perhaps, have done Galileo's work, taking a century for the task. Scholasticism was already moribund; the telescope was invented; the time was ripe; Kepler had already discovered his great laws of planetary motion; who can doubt that scholars would have arisen to fill the opening opportunity?

Gradually the fame of Galileo rose to a great height. He became the best known man in Europe. His lecture rooms were crowded. At Easter, 1610, he showed the Medicean stars to Cosmo II in Florence, and in May he writes a letter describing the work that he has projected—treatises on the constitution of the world, on mechanical motion, on sound, color, vision, tides, fortification, tactics, artillery, sieges, surveying, etc. This letter soon brought an offer from the Grand Duke to appoint Galileo first philosopher and mathematician at the University of Pisa at a salary of 1,000 scudi. He is not to be obliged to reside at Pisa—and in fact his duties were usually performed by substitutes.

In July, 1610, Galileo left the service of Venice for that of Florence. It was a sad exchange for him. Venice was the only state in Italy that dared to stand up against the power of Rome. There were weighty reasons of state why the Duke of Florence could not do so. The Jesuits had been banished from the soil of Venice (1606) 'forever.' They were all powerful in Rome and in Florence. It is evident from letters of this time that Galileo's desertion of Padua produced an unfavorable impression of self-seeking even among his friends.

Galileo's visit to Rome in March, 1611, was a veritable triumph for him. His expenses were paid by the court, he was lodged with the Tuscan ambassador, and received with the greatest honor by the Pope (Paul V.) and the cardinals, including Cardinal Barberini, the future Pope Urban VIII. To them he showed his discoveries. They were convinced and interested. At the request of Cardinal Robert Bellarmine, four learned men of the Roman College (Clavius among them) reported on what they had seen through the telescope and fully confirmed his observations. This report is of great importance, since it was, in effect, a sanction by the Church itself. Galileo was received a member of the *Accademia dei Lincei*, and its president, Prince Cesi, became his lifelong friend. The Cardinal del Monte writes to the Grand Duke of Florence (May 31, 1611) that Galileo had given great satisfaction: 'Were we still living under the ancient republic of Rome I verily believe there would have been a column on the capitol erected in his honor.' Galileo was at the top of the wave of fortune to all appearance. At this very moment, however, Cremonini's trial was going on before the Roman Inquisition and on the records is an inquiry whether Cremonini and Galileo were in any relation with each other. He was already suspected of heresy. His friendship would, even then, have been prejudicial. By 1613 Galileo was aware that there was a league of his

Florentine enemies against him. In a letter to Prince Cesi he makes light of it. 'I laugh at it,' he says, but it was none the less serious. It was based on religious scruples, but stirred to action by bitter personal animosities.

Brilliant successes, like those of Galileo, raise up an army of enemies. He was haughty with his own. Sure of his talents, his fortune and his powerful patrons in church and state, he had no managements for any one. 'The wind is fair: now is the time to take in sail,' is a maxim that he would have scorned. Of Aristotle's virtues he practised magnificence, not prudence. His colleagues in the universities were mostly Aristotelians. The heretical and Arab Aristotle had been banished; the Greek Aristotle reigned supreme. Galileo handled his opponents harshly. He was proud; he had a right to be. He was haughty; it led to his fall. When certain chosen astronomers of Italy were asked in 1615 by the Holy Office to report on his system, the report was adverse. Science and pseudo-science were in conflict and the latter won. The Aristotelianism of the universities was bound closely to that of the church. In attacking the orthodox Aristotle, Galileo attacked—or was supposed to have attacked—orthodoxy itself. His enemies were vanquished in philosophy; they dragged in texts of scripture to support the weakness of their science.

Galileo met them on this ground also, which was a fatal error. He was no more competent to discuss texts of scripture than they to decide upon points of science.

Father Castelli, an ardent friend of Galileo's, had been appointed to be professor of mathematics at Pisa (1613). At a dinner at the Ducal Palace (December, 1613) the conversation turned on astronomical matters. Did the Medicean stars really exist? asked the Dowager Duchess Christine. The professor of physics in the university reluctantly admitted that they did—that he had seen them. Castelli then praised Galileo's splendid discovery. The professor whispered something to the duchess to insinuate that while the discoveries might be true, the conclusion in favor of the Copernican theory was certainly contrary to scripture. Castelli was called upon to reply and made a brilliant answer. The Grand Duke and most of those present were convinced. Castelli reports all this to Galileo, and Galileo writes in reply (December 21, 1613) a long and eloquent letter on the subject. The original of this letter was never found, although the Inquisition made diligent search for it. Many authentic copies were circulated, however. The question of the place of the Bible in scientific questions is discussed. Galileo is a good Catholic; the scriptures cannot lie or err, he says. But the expositors are fallible. They will fall into error, nay into heresy, if they interpret Holy Writ literally. Both scriptures and external nature owe their origin to the Divine Word.

"It was necessary, however, in Holy Scripture, in order to accommodate itself to the understanding of the majority to say many things which apparently differ from the precise meaning. Nature, on the contrary, is inexorable and unchangeable, and cares not whether her hidden causes and modes of working are intelligible to the human understanding or not, and never deviates from her prescribed laws." It appears to me, therefore, says Galileo, that no effect of nature, which experience places before our eyes, or is the necessary conclusion derived from evidence, should be rendered doubtful by passages of Scripture which contain thousands of words admitting of various interpretations, for every sentence of Scripture is not bound by such rigid laws as is every effect of Nature. . . . Since two truths can obviously never contradict each other, it is the part of wise interpreters of Holy Scripture to take the pains to find out the real meaning of its statements in accordance with the conclusions regarding nature which are quite certain, either from the clear evidence of sense or from necessary demonstration. As therefore the Bible, although dictated by the Holy Spirit, admits . . . in many passages of an interpretation other than the literal one and as, moreover, we cannot maintain with certainty that all interpreters are inspired by God, I think it would be the part of wisdom not to allow anyone to apply passages of Scripture in such a way as to force them to support, as true, conclusions concerning nature, the contrary of which may afterwards be revealed by the evidences of our senses or by necessary demonstration. Who will set bounds to man's understanding? Who can assure us that everything that can be known in the world is known already? . . . I am inclined to think that the authority of Holy Writ is intended to convince men of those truths which are necessary for their salvation which, being far above man's understanding cannot be made credible by any learning, or by any other means than revelation by the Holy Spirit. But that the same God who has endowed us with senses, reason and understanding, does not permit us to use them and desires to acquaint us in any other way with such knowledge as we are in a position to acquire for ourselves by means of those faculties, that it seems to me I am not bound to believe, especially concerning those sciences about which the Holy Scriptures contain only small fragments and varying conclusions; and this is precisely the case with astronomy, of which there is so little that the planets are not even all enumerated

This noble declaration of the independence of man's reason, written in 1613, marks the highest insight yet reached by the human spirit in this regard. It is the greatest product of Galileo's philosophical genius. It was written in haste, he says, yet its form is perfect and convincing. It is the weighty expression of convictions felt, pondered over and matured. It precisely expresses the attitude of the generations that followed Darwin. No considerable body of men ever held it before that day. It delighted Castelli and a few of the more enlightened of Galileo's circle. His enemies received it with breathless, uncomprehending rage. They sought for flaws in the argument and, unhappily, they had not far to seek. For, not content with these general principles, Galileo went on to explain certain passages of scripture in a fashion that, at the best, was weak and unconvincing, almost disingenuous. The famous passage in Joshua, 'The sun stood still in the midst of heaven (and hasted not to go down about a whole day)' is expounded by first suppressing the words in parentheses, next by a wire-drawn argument to prove that Joshua's command was given when the sun was near setting (which disagrees with the words purposely omitted) and that 'the midst of heaven' does not mean the place of the sun near noon, but its central place in space among the planets. Hence, says Galileo, this passage actually demonstrates that the sun occupies the center of the world, and refutes Ptolemy. The plain meaning of the verse was distorted by a wilful suppression. It is said in the XIX. Psalm 'The sun's going forth is from the end of the heaven and his circuit unto the ends of it.' Galileo explained this to mean that the sun is the nuptial bed, and the bridegroom coming out of his chamber rejoicing is the light of the sun—his rays—not the sun himself. There is not a shade of reason for this arbitrary interpretation. It is not convincing to us; it was abhorrent to his adversaries. Is it any wonder that they loudly proclaimed their intention to protect the words of the Bible from the profane interpretations of laymen? Into the quicksand of theological interpretation Galileo had no call to enter. He should have declined the controversy thrust upon him by his enemies on the simple ground that he was no more fitted to deal with theology than his adversaries with science. This was, however, not his belief, and he accepted their challenge. By so doing he quite nullified the effect of his noble stand upon general principles. Radical and bold as this stand was, he could have maintained it as Cremonini had maintained his own upon a similar issue. At this critical point in his career two roads were open. He recklessly, even presumptuously, chose the wrong one. All his tribulations are the result of this choice. In two letters of February 16 and March 28, 1615, Galileo, writing to Mgr. Dini, regrets that he has been forced to defend his system against religious scruples. In his letter to the Grand Duchess Christine he had said 'the professors of theology should not assume authority on subjects which they have not studied.' It never so much as crossed his mind that his own interpretations of the texts of Joshua and the Psalms were like assumptions of authority. In all that follows it must not be forgotten that Galileo had the free choice of leaving the scriptural interpretations alone and of confining himself to science and to philosophical considerations of a general nature. He *chose* to enter the lists, and there is every reason to believe that he felt sure of winning.

Galileo's case recalls that of Roger Bacon, nearly four centuries earlier. The science of both these men of genius was, in the main and essentially, illuminating and correct. It was, for both of them, opposed by ignorant men who feared that which they could not understand. Both of them went out of the province in which alone they had authority, to enter another in which their contemporaries and fellows were at least as well able to judge as they. Both of them overbore and offended their colleagues by harshness. When they were brought to trial those very colleagues were, in turn, accusers, jurors and judges. A like fate befell both.

The history of Jordano Bruno does not fall within the scope of this article and need be considered only so far as it affected the contemporaries of Galileo, and Galileo himself. The following paragraphs from Draper's

'Intellectual Development of Europe' give the views of a writer who is inclined to present Bruno's history in the most favorable light. The foot notes are my own.

Against the opposition it had to encounter, the heliocentric theory made its way slowly at first. Among those who did adopt it were some whose connection served rather to retard its progress, because of the ultraism of their views, or the doubtfulness of their social position. Such was Bruno, who contributed largely to its introduction into England, and who was the author of a work on the Plurality of Worlds, and of the conception that every star is a sun, having opaque planets revolving about it—a conception to which the Copernican system suggestively leads. Bruno was born (1550) seven years after the death of Copernicus. He became a Dominican, but, like so many other thoughtful men of the times, was led into heresy on the doctrine of transubstantiation. Not concealing his opinions he was persecuted, fled, and led a vagabond life in foreign countries, testifying that wherever he went he found scepticism under the polish of hypocrisy, and that he fought not against the belief of men, but against their pretended belief. For teaching the rotation of the earth he had to flee to Switzerland, and thence to England, where, at Oxford, he gave lectures on Cosmology. Driven from England, France and Germany in succession, he ventured in his extremity to return to Italy, and was arrested in Venice where he was kept in prison in the Piombi for six years without books, or paper, or friends. Meantime the Inquisition demanded him as having written heretical works. He was therefore surrendered to Rome, and, after a further imprisonment of two years, tried, excommunicated, and delivered over to the secular authorities, to be punished 'as mercifully as possible and without the shedding of his blood,' the abominable formula for burning a man alive. He had collected all the observations that had been made respecting the new star in Cassiopeia, 1572; he had taught that space is infinite, and that it is filled with self-luminous and opaque worlds many of them inhabited—this being his capital offense. He believed that the world is animated by an intelligent soul, the cause of forms but not of matter; that it lives in all things, even such as seem not to live; that everything is ready to become organized; that matter is the mother of forms and then their grave; that matter and the soul of the world together constitute God. His ideas were therefore pantheistic, 'Est Deus in nobis.' In his *Cena delle Cenere* he insists that the Scripture was not intended to teach science, but morals only. The severity with which he was treated was provoked by his asseverations that he was struggling with an orthodoxy that had neither morality nor belief. This was the aim of his work entitled 'The Triumphant Beast.' He was burned at Rome, February 16, 1600.

In 1612 Galileo writes to Kepler that epicycles and eccentrics are not chimerical; 'not only are there many motions in eccentrics and epicycles, but there are no other motions.' This, written three years after Kepler had sent him his Theory of Mars containing the proof of elliptic motion, shows that Galileo had not yet appreciated Kepler's revolutionary discoveries. It is doubtful if he ever did so. He makes no effective use of them in his arguments in favor of the Copernican doctrines.

In the meantime busy enemies were stirring up trouble. The letter to Castelli gave great offense. The Bishop of Fiesole became enraged at Copernicus and was much surprised to learn that he had been dead for eighty years. A Dominican friar, P. Caccini, preached a violent sermon against Galileo (1614) on the text *Viri Galilæi quid statis aspicientes in cœlum?* Ye men of Galilee, why stand ye gazing up into Heaven? Castelli was advised by the archbishop of Pisa, 'for his welfare,' 'if he wished to escape ruin,' to abandon the Copernican opinion, because that opinion, besides being an absurdity, was perilous, scandalous, rash, heretical and contrary to scripture.

Another Dominican friar, Lorini, addressed to Cardinal Mellini, president of the Congregation of the Index, a denunciation of 'the Galileists,' who hold the doctrine of Copernicus. The congregation accordingly (February, 1619) opened a secret inquiry. A copy of Galileo's letter to Castelli was examined by the consultator of the Holy Office, who pronounced that some phrases of it looked ill at first sight, but that they were capable of interpretation in a good sense, and did not deviate from Catholic doctrine. Caccini was summoned to Rome as a witness and gave evidence, most of which was found to be baseless (November, 1615) and was disregarded.

Early in the same year Galileo had sent copies of the letter to Castelli to friends in Rome. It was greatly admired; but his friends, one and all, strenuously advised him to keep to philosophy and to avoid religious discussion. Prince Cesi expressly warns him to avoid all mention of the Copernican theory, for Cardinal Bellarmine—a good, great and powerful prince of the Church—had told him that in his opinion the theory was heretical and contrary to scripture. Cardinals Barberini, Del Monte and Bellarmine assured Galileo's Roman friends that so long as he confined himself to scientific questions and did not enter into theological interpretations of the Bible he had nothing to fear (August, 1615). All these cardinals were very friendly to Galileo personally, and their friendship stood him in good stead. Their attitude was representative of that of the church. So long as religion was not attacked science was to be free. Any assault on doctrine was to be repelled with vigor, and at all costs.

Theological interpretation was not to be permitted to laymen. That was a business reserved by the church.

A Carmelite monk, Foscarini, printed in 1615 a letter on 'the opinion of the Pythagoreans and of Copernicus of the mobility of the earth and the stability of the sun,' which was widely read and quickly came to a second edition. The Inquisition was at this time considering Foscarini's book also. Galileo felt that his presence at Rome would be advantageous, and in December, 1615, he set out provided with letters of introduction from the Grand Duke to dignitaries, including the Tuscan ambassador, Guicciardini. He was received with honor as a celebrity. With no great effort he freed himself from all personal difficulties and was able to report (February 6, 1616) that the monk Caccini had made him a formal visit to ask his pardon. On the same day he writes to the Tuscan Secretary of State, Piechena: "My business, so far as it relates to myself, is completed. All the exalted personages who have been conducting it have told me so plainly and in a most obliging manner. . . . So far as this point is concerned, therefore, I might return home without delay."

He goes on to say that it is proposed to pass judgment upon the Copernician doctrine, and that it is his conviction that he may be of use in the investigation of the matter, on account of his scientific knowledge. Accordingly he proposes to stay. He had been personally vindicated. It was his ardent desire to convert the Romans to the heliocentric theory. This he attempted by giving private lectures in many of the great houses of Rome. His lectures began by stating all the arguments in favor of Ptolemy's system and then went on to demolish them one by one, leaving nothing standing. The lectures were admired by many great folk, and Galileo gained a great personal success for the time. His very success made his well-wishers uneasy and unquiet.

Before Galileo's visit, Fra Paolo Sarpi, professor of philosophy in Venice, distinguished as a champion of free thought and as a friend of Galileo had written: "I hear that Galileo is going to Rome, where he is invited by several Cardinals to explain his new discoveries in the heavens. I fear much that, in such a case, he may develop the reasons that lead him to prefer the doctrine of Copernicus, which will be far from pleasing to the Jesuits and other monks. They have changed what was only a question of physics and astronomy into a theological question, and I foresee, with great vexation, that Galileo, in order to live in peace, and not labeled as heretic and excommunicate, will be constrained to abjure his real sentiments on this matter. A day will come, of that I am almost sure, when enlightened men will deplore the misfortune of Galileo and the injustice done to so great a man. But, pending that day, he must suffer, and he must not complain otherwise than secretly."

The Tuscan ambassador at Rome was anxious to be rid of Galileo, and in many letters reports that it were well he returned home. He hints that Galileo's course may even bring dangers to Tuscany; he cannot 'approve that we should expose ourselves to such annoyances and dangers without very good reason.' He insinuates that Cardinal Carlo de Medici may be compromised (March 4, 1616). "Galileo seems disposed to emulate the monks in obstinacy, and to contend with personages who cannot be attacked without ruining yourself; we shall soon hear at Florence that he has madly tumbled into some abyss or other." "The moment is badly chosen to promulgate a philosophical idea." The Grand Duke, from friendliness to Galileo and in fear of untoward complications, gave instructions for his recall, which were conveyed in a dispatch from the ducal secretary: "You have had enough of monkish persecutions. . . . His Highness fears that your longer tarrying at Rome might involve you in difficulties, and would therefore be glad, as you have so far come honorably out of the affair, if you would not tease the sleeping dog any more, and would return here as soon as possible. For there are rumors flying about which we do not like, and the monks are all powerful." Galileo set out for Florence on the fourth of April, 1616.

Let us stop for a moment to inquire what the course of affairs would have been if Galileo, whose personal affairs were honorably concluded on February 6, had thereupon returned to Florence. He had renewed old friendships; he had formed new ones; he was esteemed and regarded by the Pope and the most influential of the Cardinals. His enemies in Florence were utterly silenced. His accuser, Caccini, had made the humblest apologies. The Grand Duke and most of the court were his admiring friends. He had every freedom for research if only he would leave the interpretation of scripture to theological experts. 'Write freely, but keep outside the sacristy' his friends advised. Why did he remain in Rome? To convert the Congregation of the Index to Copernicanism? This would have been a triumph for science, and a personal triumph as well. The Roman Curia had absolutely no interest in science as such. They were determined that religion should not suffer. Galileo's brilliant lectures were not conceived in the spirit that convinces. He silenced opposition by sarcasm. A second crisis in Galileo's affairs dates from this period (February, March, 1615).

Before this date momentous action had been taken by the Inquisition. On February 19 the Qualificators of the Holy Office had been summoned to give their opinion on two propositions based on Galileo's treatise on the Solar Spots:

I. That the sun is the center of the world and immovable from its place.

II. That the earth is not the center of the world, nor immovable, but moves, and also with a diurnal motion.

The Qualificators were to give their opinion as theological and philosophical experts, and gave it four days afterwards. The astronomer Riccioli declares that the opinions of astronomical experts were also obtained and that the judgment of the Holy Office was based upon them (Delambre: *Histoire de l'Astronomie Moderne*, i., 680). There is no reason to doubt the assertion. It is exceedingly important as showing that the Inquisition took the best expert advice known to them before action. This significant fact is not mentioned in any of the Warfare-of-Science books, nor even by so careful an historian as Gebler.

The scientific value of the expert astronomical opinion was, of course, exactly *nil*. It was given, probably, by Aristotelians, personally inimical to Galileo, and fully committed to the Ptolemaic system. It was, equally of course, adverse to Galileo. They may well have quoted the dictum of Tycho Brahe that the system of Copernicus was 'absurd and contrary to Holy Writ' since the judgment recites these very words. On March 5, 1616, the 'De Revolutionibus' of Copernicus and another work by Diego di Zuniga were suspended by the Congregation of the Index 'until they be corrected,' and Foscarini's book was 'altogether prohibited and condemned' as well as 'all other works' in which the Copernican opinion is taught. On February 25 the Pope directed 'Cardinal Bellarmine to summon before him the said Galileo and to admonish him to abandon the said opinion; and, in case of his refusal to obey, that the Commissary is to intimate to him, before a notary and witnesses, a command to abstain altogether from teaching or defending this opinion and doctrine, and even from discussing it; and if he do not acquiesce therein, that he is to be imprisoned.' This document is followed in the Vatican MS. by another: "Friday, the 26th (February, 1616). At the Palace, the usual residence of the Lord Cardinal Bellarmine, the said Galileo, having been summoned and brought before the said Lord Cardinal, was in the presence of the Most Rev'd Michael Angelo Segnezzio, . . . Commissary-General of the Holy Office, by the said Cardinal warned of the error of the aforesaid opinion and admonished to abandon it; and immediately thereafter, before me and before witnesses, the Lord Cardinal Bellarmine being still present, the said Galileo was by the said Commissary commanded and enjoined . . . to relinquish altogether the said opinion . . . ; nor henceforth to hold, teach or defend it in any way whatsoever, verbally or in writing; otherwise proceedings would be taken against him in the Holy Office; which injunction the said Galileo acquiesced in and promised to obey. Done at Rome in the place above said, in presence of (two persons named) witnesses." This annotation was long supposed to have been fabricated in 1632 to meet new conditions then arising. It is, however, entirely genuine. (Gebler's 'Galileo,' Appendix III.)

The exact wording is to be noted. Upon this admonition the subsequent fate of Galileo hangs.

Chapter III

An extant annotation dated February 26, 1616, which is undoubtedly genuine, declares that upon this day Galileo was summoned before Cardinal Bellarmine and in the presence of witnesses was warned of the error of the Copernican opinion taught by him, and was admonished henceforth not to hold, teach or defend it in any way whatsoever, verbally or in writing . . . which injunction the said Galileo promised to obey. The exact wording should be noticed. Upon it the subsequent fate of Galileo hangs. The document is genuine. Does it represent the facts of his examination of 1616 exactly as they occurred?

The proceedings against Galileo in 1632-3 show that the Pope and the Holy Office acted precisely as if the statements of the annotation were exact. The publication of his *Dialogues* (1631) was a *flagrant* violation of the command not to teach, etc. In the case of a personage so celebrated as Galileo nothing less than a flagrant violation would be noticed. The Roman Curia could not afford to harass him about trifles. With his defense of 1633 he submitted the following certificate:

We, Roberto Cardinal Bellarmine, having heard that it is calumniously reported that Signor Galileo Galilei has in our hand abjured and has also been punished with salutary penance, and being requested to state the truth as to this, declare: that the said Signor Galileo has not abjured . . . any opinion or doctrine held by him, neither has any salutary penance been imposed upon him; but only the declaration made by the Holy Father and published by the Sacred Congregation of the Index has been intimated to him, wherein it is set forth that the doctrine attributed to Copernicus, . . . is contrary to the Holy Scriptures and therefore cannot be defended or held. In witness whereof we have written and subscribed these presents with our hand this 26th day of May, 1616. Roberto Card. Bellarmino.

Galileo's enemies had spread the calumnious reports mentioned. He wished to have a proof that they were false. Cardinal Bellarmine was his friend and admirer and at his request gave this certificate. Bellarmine died in 1621 and could not be called as a witness in 1632. When Galileo was called upon to defend himself for teaching the Copernican doctrine in his *Dialogues*, which had given great offense, he produced this certificate and called attention to its wording, which differs materially from that of the protocol of February 26, being much less stringent in form. In essence it is the same; to teach a doctrine as true is to 'defend' it. Cardinal Bellarmine did not have the protocol before him in writing the informal certificate. The prohibition of the latter is, however, precise and absolute; the doctrine 'cannot be defended,' that is, taught in any way as if it were true. It cannot even be 'held,' silently. It represented the attitude of the cardinal's mind precisely; the church would not suffer if its terms were obeyed. In reading Galileo's defense of 1632-3, we shall see the use he made of the discrepancy between these two documents, one formal and of record (February 26), the other friendly and informal (May 26).

It is the theory of Gebler in his careful history, 'Galileo Galilei and the Roman Curia,' that the genuine document of February 26 is not a true record of the facts. He admits that it was written in its proper place by the notary. He finds an 'obvious contradiction' between a formal command 'not in any way to hold or defend,' which are the words of the process of 1633, and the prohibition of Bellarmine's certificate 'not to defend or hold.' After an examination of all the documents it is impossible, I think, to take Gebler's view. It is necessary to admit the words of the genuine documents to mean precisely what they say.

Gebler lays down three facts as indisputable: '(I.) Galileo did not receive any prohibition except the cardinal's admonition not to defend or hold the Copernican doctrine; (II.) Entire silence on the subject was therefore not enjoined upon him; (III.) The second part of the note in the Vatican MS. of February 26, 1616, is therefore untrue.' My own conclusions are entirely different as to all three prohibitions. The Cardinal's admonitions are, in effect, absolutely the same as those of the formal prohibition; silence was enjoined, and more than this Galileo was forbidden to hold certain opinions even mentally and silently. If not, what does Bellarmine mean by the word 'hold'? Is it, I ask, credible that an authority that forbids a man to hold an opinion, even silently, would permit him to teach it? To ask the question is to answer it. When Galileo taught the opinion he disobeyed the orders of a Church whose authority he fully admitted during the whole of his life.

Within the assigned limits of this paper the matter cannot be discussed at length. Two points may be touched upon however. Galileo's letters to Florence in 1616 do not mention the prohibition to himself for two good reasons, *first*, to divulge the proceedings of the Holy Office would have been a serious matter; *second*, Galileo had every reason for convincing his friends that the Holy Office had only come to decisions 'purely public' regarding the Copernican doctrine, and 'not affecting my [his] personal interests' (letter of March 6, 1616).

Again, the protocol of February 25 gives the orders of the Pope that certain things should be done 'in case of his refusal to obey.' It does not explicitly enjoin or prohibit the same action after his promise of obedience. Cardinal Bellarmine had full power in such a matter. If Galileo had refused to obey he would have been imprisoned. When he had promised to abandon the opinion of Copernicus the obvious step for Cardinal Bellarmine was to bind him to effective silence by a formal promise before witnesses. The protocol of February 26 recites that this was done. The words mean, I am obliged to conclude, precisely what they say. It must not be forgotten that Galileo, like every other good Catholic, had been forbidden to hold the Copernican opinion by the general prohibition of March 5, 1616.

The reigning Pope was Paul V., who hated 'science and polite scholars.' He was very civil to Galileo, however, received him graciously (March 11, 1616) and promised him safety from his enemies. Galileo was a celebrity; by his submission to authority he had averted a great scandal in the church; accordingly the Pope was gracious. For the next seven years (1616-23) Galileo's conduct precisely agrees with the supposition that he recognized that he must not teach the Copernican doctrines. He published nothing during this period. The authorities at Rome were engaged in 'correcting' the work of Copernicus. Galileo eagerly waited for the corrections, for they would be authoritative and would exhibit the limits within which it would be permitted to 'teach.'

In May, 1618, he sent a MS. copy of his treatise on the tides to Archduke Leopold of Austria, who was friendly to him. It implicitly assumes the truth of the Copernican doctrine "which I then (1616) held to be true until it pleased those gentlemen to prohibit the work and to declare that opinion (of Copernicus) to be false and contrary to Scripture. Now, knowing as I do, that it behoves us to obey the decisions of the authorities, and to believe them, since they are guided by a higher insight than any to which my humble mind can attain, I consider this treatise which I send you merely to be a poetical conceit, or a dream, and desire that your Highness may take it as such . . . ." The words are ironical. They will have less effect upon us when we remember that the science of this treatise of Galileo's is quite erroneous. It denies that the moon controls the tides. The treatise was not published. It was shown in MS. to a few trusted friends, but the ideas here set forth were developed in Galileo's *Dialogues* published in 1632.

In 1618 three comets appeared in the sky. Galileo communicated his views of their nature to a few friends. He considered them to be merely atmospheric appearances which rise far beyond the moon, to be sure, and not heavenly bodies. The conclusion was erroneous, of course. In 1619 the Jesuit Father Grassi delivered a lecture in Rome maintaining that the comets were heavenly bodies (as they are). Galileo induced one of his pupils to reply to Grassi, and himself corrected the MS. work so that its severe criticisms of the Jesuit (who was, after all, defending a true thesis) are Galileo's own. A reply was written by Grassi in which Galileo is personally attacked and the Copernican system assailed. Galileo's answer is the famous *Il Saggiatore* (the assayer) which was printed October, 1623. It was brilliantly, but very carefully written, and before it was published it passed from hand to hand among Galileo's friends, who purged it of every phrase likely to be dangerous. The *imprimatur* was given on a report of Father Riccardi, a former pupil of Galileo's, of whom we shall hear more.

In July Pope Gregory XV. died and was succeeded by Urban VIII. who, as Cardinal Maffeo Barberini, had for many years been one of Galileo's strongest supporters. A new era seemed to open with his accession. His many letters to Galileo had always been friendly, often cordial. In thanking Galileo for his letters on solar spots (1613) the cardinal had written: "I shall not fail to read them with pleasure, again and again, which they deserve. . . . I thank you very much for your remembrance of me, and beg you not to forget the high opinion that I entertain for a mind so extraordinarily gifted as yours." In 1620 the cardinal composed a poem in Galileo's honor and sent it to him as a 'proof of great affection.'

During the progress of Galileo's affair with the Holy Office in 1615 and 1616, the cardinal stood his friend and believed that it was chiefly to his own efforts that an issue so satisfactory to the astronomer personally was brought about. He was a friend to Galileo; he was not a believer in the Copernican doctrine; he made no efforts to prevent its condemnation. He proved to be inexorable where the interests of the papacy were, or seemed to be, involved. His accession was hailed by Galileo's friends, and *Il Saggiatore* was dedicated to him, and he accepted the dedication. The book is considered a model of dialectic skill and a literary masterpiece. The original controversy about the comets is almost lost sight of. The errors of Grassi are shown up mercilessly. The Copernican system, which Galileo 'as a pious

Catholic considers entirely erroneous and completely denies' is covertly defended. It is shown to agree with the revelations of the telescope; and these are proved to be inexplicable on any other system. As the Copernican opinion is, however, condemned by the church, as Ptolemy's is untenable, and Tycho's inadequate, Galileo concludes that some other system must be sought for.

In this brilliant essay—which was withheld until Galileo's powerful friend was seated in the pontifical chair—Galileo held, taught and defended the Copernican doctrine. It was supposed to be, at least, safe for him to do so in a covert way. The book was read by the Pope, who enjoyed it highly—so Galileo heard. It was examined by the Inquisition and no action was taken. By these and other signs Galileo judged that an attempt to remove the condemnation of the Copernican system might now, at least, succeed. Its weightiest opponent, Cardinal Bellarmine, an earnest, sincere and learned man, had died in 1621. Galileo proposed to go to Rome to congratulate the new Pope on his accession. The proposal was well received. Friends wrote to him: "I swear to you that nothing pleased his holiness so much as the mention of your name . . . the Pope replied that it would give him great pleasure, . . . if the journey would not be injurious to your health;

for great men like you must spare themselves that they may live as long as possible."

Galileo arrived in Rome towards the end of April, 1624. He was received with the greatest honor. Everyone knew the Pope to be his friend and that he had many supporters among notabilities. In the space of six weeks he was granted six long audiences with the pontiff. The Copernican system was discussed. Galileo argued warmly in its favor. He met with no success, while the Pope replied with arguments of his own against it. The new doctrine was not to be tolerated. Certain of the cardinals, at Galileo's request, engaged in the matter. The Pope was inexorable. No one can decide now what the Pope's arguments were. From the whole course of events, it seems probable that he was not satisfied that the Copernican theory was true; and it is evident that his mind was made up to allow no scandal to arise from its teaching. Galileo returned home loaded with favors. A pension was promised to his son. The Pope gave him a splendid picture, and two medals, and furthermore addressed a letter to the Grand Duke of Tuscany (June 7, 1624) in which he declares that Galileo's great discoveries 'will shine on earth so long as Jupiter and his satellites shine in heaven.' 'That you may fully understand to what extent he is dear to us, we wish to give this brilliant testimony to his virtues and piety.' 'We have observed in him not only literary distinction, but also the love of religion and all the good qualities worthy of the papal favor.'

Galileo was again at the very summit of prosperity. He thought it safe, on his return to Florence, to write a reply to an Italian advocate, Ingoli, in which he defends the Copernican theory. In the first place he shows that he formerly defended it because of its inherent probability. He proves that he had not defended an idea improbable or unreasonable in itself. Again he desires to show the Protestant Copernicans in Germany that the heliocentric doctrine had not been rejected in Italy from ignorance of its great probability, but from reverence for Holy Scripture, zeal for religion and our holy faith.

Il Saggiatore had been well received. Why might he not go further under the favor of the Pope? All reports from Rome were favorable. And indeed he had heard (December, 1625) that the Pope had listened to several passages from this last pamphlet and had highly approved them. If he had gone so far, why then might he not go still farther? On the surface of affairs there was no apparent reason. Up to this time Galileo had preserved the forms fully. He professed not to hold Copernican doctrines. Not holding them, how could his writings be taken as teaching or defending them? The Pope, his friend, had not disapproved his previous writings. Galileo misinterpreted this as a sign of his toleration of the doctrines. It is now apparent that the Pope's whole course was consistent. He desired to give Galileo every liberty, but was sternly set against any teachings that would diminish the authority of the Church. From first to last he was unconvinced of the scientific truth of the Copernican opinion. He had personally befriended and honored Galileo. He looked for a grateful acknowledgment in return. Galileo had been denounced by his enemies, but they were overawed, and would certainly take up no quarrel in which he was not flagrantly disobedient to the prohibition of 1616. *Il Saggiatore* had been a brilliant success. He now set about arranging another work—the *Dialogues on the two principal systems of the World*—parts of which had been in hand for some years.

This is the place to record Galileo's share in the invention of the microscope. While he was in Rome (1624) a complicated microscope was shown to him that had been invented by Drebbel, a Dutchman. Galileo simplified and greatly improved it. His relation to the invention of the telescope and of the microscope is the same. The first ideas came from others; Galileo put them into practical forms. The real inventor of the microscope is not Drebbel, but Zacharias Jansen, a spectacle maker of Middleburg who made the first instruments in the last years of the sixteenth century, before the telescope was invented, therefore.

Galileo's dialogues on the system of the world (1632) have, at the head, a Greek epigraph:

In Every Judgment beware of Your Prejudices!

They are dedicated to the Grand Duke of Tuscany. The personages of the *Dialogues* are Salviati (Galileo himself) who maintains the Copernican doctrines; Sangredo, a man-of-the-world, intelligent, but not a savant; and Simplicius, a convinced Aristotelian, a dull fellow, always worsted in the argument. Galileo's enemies convinced the Pope that Simplicius stood for the Pontiff himself. The subjects discussed are the fall of bodies, the flight of projectiles, the principles of mechanics, the rotation and revolution of the earth and of the planets, the system of Ptolemy—and here Sangredo remarks that he knows many disciples of Ptolemy who have become Copernicans, but not one Copernican converted to the ancient system. The new star of 1572 is shown to have been far more distant than the moon, by long calculations (and it is noteworthy that logarithms are not employed to shorten the work). The preface recites that, some years previously a 'salutary edict' had been promulgated at Rome which, to prevent scandals, forbade the teaching of the Pythagorean opinion of the earth's motion, that some hardy spirits had, nevertheless, dared to declare that this edict had been issued without comprehension of the matter and that it was the result of passion, and not of judicial examination. It had been said that advisers entirely ignorant of astronomy ought not to have thus clipped the wings of philosophers.

My zeal, says Galileo, cannot support these rash complaints. Well understanding this prudent decree, I wish to do justice to the truth. I was then at Rome; the most distinguished prelates heard and applauded me; the decree would not have been issued without giving me some knowledge of it. I, therefore, wish to show to foreign nations that in Italy, and even at Rome, all that could be advanced in favor of Copernicus was known, before that censure was published. I declared myself the advocate of Copernicus. Proceeding according to a mathematical hypothesis, I endeavored to prove it to be preferable to that which declares the earth at rest, not in an absolute manner preferable, but in the sense in which it is attacked by pretended Aristotelians, who in their philosophizing neglect observations. He will show, he says, certain advantages of the heliocentric system. If Italians have not assented to the mathematical opinion of the motion of the earth, it is not because all of them have been ignorant of the reasons others allege in its support, but because they have other reasons based on piety, religion, on a knowledge of divine omnipotence and the weakness of the human understanding. It is the opinion of good authorities that the foregoing introduction was first written by Galileo, then revised by the censor at Rome—perhaps by the Pope himself—and finally returned to the author with permission to make such verbal changes as would not alter the sense of the Roman revision.

In the *Dialogues* the three interlocutors proceed to construct a scheme of the universe, step by step. The construction is made by Simplicius, and the system proposed by Copernicus and demonstrated by Galileo emerges triumphant. All the glory is for Copernicus and his advocate, Galileo. No credit is assigned to Kepler for his discoveries which had done away with the whole apparatus of epicycles retained by Copernicus. Kepler is not mentioned here or elsewhere with praise.

Simplicius objects to some mathematical reasoning because Aristotle recommended his disciples to abstain from geometry. Salviati thinks Aristotle wise; for geometry is the art by which his errors and deceits are discovered. As to the empty spaces beyond Saturn: who are we to judge of the greatness of the universe? Can we say that these spaces are useless because we see no planet there? May they not be peopled with invisible planets? Who suspected the existence of the moons of Jupiter? Who tells us that all the heavenly bodies were created for us? Certain authors—Kepler, for one—assert that tides are caused by the moon. Galileo will not waste his time in refuting such assertions. Nothing is so astonishing to Galileo as that Kepler, a free and penetrating spirit, should have assented to such 'ineptitudes.' Simplicius on his part declares that the tides are miracles. In all the book there is no discussion of Scriptural texts.

It is not necessary to carry the analysis of these famous dialogues further. The arguments employed are so familiar to us that we forget they were once fresh and novel. They were accepted by Galileo's contemporaries as witty and brilliant, and even now Italians admire their style, though most English readers find them, as a whole, prolix, not to say dull. The Copernican doctrine is enforced in every possible way.

Every argument for the Aristotelian theory is brought forward, in turn, by Simplicius only to be utterly refuted. Sarcasm is unsparingly employed. Simplicius is not only wrong, but ludicrously so. After each unusually convincing passage Salviati is careful to add that, after all, the Copernican doctrine is a 'fantasy' or a 'vain chimera.' At the termination of the dialogues, which extend over four days, no general summing-up is made. The reader is left to draw his own conclusions. Salviati apologizes to Simplicius for the ardor of his language and assures him that he had no intention to offend him, but wished rather to stimulate him to communicate his 'sublime' ideas—ideas which have been utterly refuted in the course of the book. 'Your reasons,' says Simplicius, 'are most ingenious; but I do not believe them to be either true or conclusive.' Then Simplicius recalls a wise reflection, made formerly, in his presence, by an eminent personage before whom all must bow, as follows: 'We observe,' he says, 'nothing but appearances; by what right do you presume to limit the power of God by fixing the ways in which it has pleased Him to produce them?' These are the very words spoken by Pope Urban to Galileo in 1624. They were considered conclusive by the Pope. In the mouth of Simplicius they ring hollow.

It must not be forgotten that Galileo's theory of the tides upon which the *Dialogues* turn is, in itself, entirely erroneous. The tides are not due to the moon, he says, but to certain motions of the earth, which are then discussed. The first motion is its rotation round an axis, the second its motion of revolution about the sun, and there is a third motion by virtue of which its axis of rotation is constrained to pass always through the same stars. The third motion (invented by Copernicus) is superfluous. The axis of the earth is always parallel to itself as it moves round the sun. Two motions are sufficient to account for all the phenomena; the third does not exist. It was, however, upon this third motion that Galileo founded his theory of the tides, which is, therefore, baseless. Many of his arguments for the Copernican doctrine are irresistible. Those founded on the tides are, necessarily, erroneous.

To obtain the authority to print the *Dialogues* Galileo went to Rome (May, 1630), where his friend and former pupil, Father Riccardi, was censor (master of the Sacred Palace). Without the *imprimatur* nothing could be printed. When the *imprimatur* of the censor was once given to any book its author was *prima facie* relieved from responsibility. In the subsequent proceedings against Galileo it was charged that he obtained the *imprimatur* by a 'ruse.' The history, as understood at Rome, was briefly as follows: In May, 1630, Galileo took the MS. to Rome, submitted it to the master of the Sacred Palace (Riccardi) and asked permission to print. Riccardi wished, for greater security, to review the book himself. To save time, it was agreed that the book should be printed at once and that the sheets, leaf by leaf, should be sent to Riccardi. To carry out this plan the *imprimatur* was given for Rome. Galileo soon went to Florence and from thence asked the censor for permission to print at Florence. This permission was refused. Riccardi insisted that the sheets should be submitted to him according to the original agreement. The plague was then raging throughout Italy and it was impossible to transmit parcels from Florence to Rome on account of the quarantine.

It was finally arranged through the Tuscan ambassador, Niccolini, that the printing should be done at Florence under the condition of the submission of the whole work to a competent theologian of the Benedictine order, and that the introduction and conclusion should be sent, before issue, to the censor at Rome. The whole matter was then transferred to the inquisitor at Florence and the book was printed with the entire approval of Father Stephani, who had been charged with its supervision. The introduction and conclusion were duly sent to Rome, but the Roman censor kept them for months without giving his approval or, in fact, without communicating with Galileo. It was clear that Riccardi was doubtful. Through the Tuscan ambassador at Rome renewed efforts were made by Galileo to obtain Riccardi's approval, and, in the meantime, without waiting for it (March 1631) the printing was proceeded with at Florence. Riccardi (April 28, 1631) at last answered Galileo's request, refusing the *imprimatur* until new conditions had been fulfilled. The censor, in this letter, recalled the fact that this original *imprimatur* was only given conditionally.

"Father Stephani," says the censor, "has no doubt subjected the book to a conscientious revision; but as he was not acquainted with the Pope's views he had no power to give any approval, etc." A desire to delay the whole matter is evident. Riccardi fears for himself; he knows the Pope's views; he is a firm friend of Galileo's also. After further negotiations (May, 1631) the whole matter was referred to the inquisitor at Florence with full powers. Riccardi conveyed to the inquisitor the 'views' that must govern his decision: The Copernican system must be treated only as a mathematical hypothesis; there must be no reference to Scripture; the introduction and the conclusion of the book the censor will send from Rome. Accordingly, they were sent with permission to Galileo to change the rhetorical style but not the matter. It is the opinion of certain good authorities that the Pope himself revised the introduction. The book was finally printed (February, 1632) with the *imprimatur* of Rome and also of Florence. The authorities at Rome had not seen the text of the *Dialogues*. It appears that throughout the long and vexatious delays Galileo obeyed all explicit instructions given by the censors. There were good reasons for removing the printing of the work to Florence. It is, however, certain that it would never have been authorized in Rome in its final shape.

Chapter IV

When the master of the palace examined the published book he discovered that Galileo had not obeyed the orders and injunctions given to him by the Holy Office on February 26, 1616, sixteen years previously. Therefore the *imprimatur* for Rome was wrongly attached. Galileo did not inform the Inquisitor at Florence of the aforesaid injunctions and orders. Therefore the *imprimatur* for Florence was obtained by a 'ruse.' Such was substantially the theory held by Galileo's judges at Rome. It was, in strictness, true. The command of the Holy Office (February 26, 1616) not to hold, teach or defend the Copernican opinion had been violated in the *Dialogues* (as indeed it had been violated less flagrantly in *Il Saggiatore* and in the letter on the tides). The orders of Riccardi were obeyed in form but not in substance. If the text of the *Dialogues* had been submitted at Rome, the Roman *imprimatur* would never have been given.

Finally, the general prohibition of March 5, 1616, not to teach the Copernican opinion had been disobeyed in the *Dialogues,* as in the two preceding publications. That no proceedings had been taken regarding the two last-named books did not in their eyes excuse the issuance of the former.

If Galileo had merely desired to promulgate the Copernican truths it would have been perfectly easy and safe for him to have printed his book in Germany, with or without his name. But he wished for an Italian triumph even more than for the spreading of a doctrine that he knew to be true.

The *Dialogues* were received on all hands with the greatest interest. Galileo's friends were delighted as they before had been with *Il Saggiatore*. They expected a similar reception for his new book, and Galileo beyond a doubt shared their expectations. Castelli—who was in favor with the Pope, and in Rome—wrote that he should read nothing else but the *Dialogues* and his Breviary. The enemies of Galileo were for the moment paralyzed with anxiety and rage. The arguments of the *Dialogues* were more dangerous than those of *Il Saggiatore* even. Its attack on Aristotelianism and orthodoxy was even more insidious and vigorous. The upper classes of Italy have always keenly relished irony and sarcasm. They were now laughing openly at the overthrow of the scholastics. The universities, the Jesuits and many of the clergy, on the other hand, were solidly arrayed against Galileo. The Jesuits were especially inimical. In a juncture like this everything depended upon the Pope. Galileo confidently expected his support, but he had misread the Pope's mind from the very first. The Pope was surrounded by Galileo's enemies. Every point that would tell was made against the book and its author. The dangers that lurked in the Copernican doctrine were exposed; Galileo's former interpretations of Holy Writ were set forth as monstrous, coming, as they did, from the pen of a layman; their obvious weaknesses were pointed out; he was denounced as a rebel to church authority, which had forbidden any one to teach the Copernican doctrine (March 5, 1616); the Pope was convinced that Galileo had intended to portray him in the character of Simplicius.

It is absolutely certain that Galileo had no such intention. Under the circumstances it would have been madness for him to alienate his powerful friend and patron. Exactly why he closed his *Dialogues* with the quotation of the Pope's own words (spoken to Galileo in 1624) it is impossible to say. To us, in the light of events, the quotation seems an inconceivable blunder. But Galileo was very far from a blunderer. He was skilled in fine logic and with his pen. The closing words of the *Dialogues* (containing the quotation) can be read so as to express a humble submission to authority. It was beyond a doubt, Galileo's intention that they should be so read; it is equally certain that the submission was only perfunctory; the reckless irony of all that preceded them made the quoted words appear as mere foolishness in the mouth of the foolish Simplicius. The very name—Simplicius—was offensive to the Pope. It was not until after July, 1636, that he expressed himself as convinced that Galileo had intended no disrespect. It was then too late. On July 26, 1636, Galileo writes: "I hear from Rome that his Eminence Cardinal Antonio Barberini and the French ambassador (de Noailles) have seen his Holiness and tried to convince him that I never had the least idea of perpetrating so sacrilegious an act as to make game of his Holiness, as my malicious foes have persuaded him, which has been the prime cause of all my troubles." The *prime* cause was Urban's conviction that Galileo had brought scandal into the church by teaching a doctrine which was, as yet, unproved.

The storm was about to break. From now onward the story is fully told in the official documents of the inquisition. The further sale of the *Dialogues* was prohibited. Galileo's conduct was referred to a special commission of theologians and men versed in science to investigate. That it was not directly sent to the Holy Office was a signal mark of favor. A letter, drawn up by Galileo, was despatched by the Grand Duke to the angry Pope. On September 4, 1632, the Pope said to the Tuscan ambassador, Niccolini—Galileo's faithful friend: 'Your Galileo has ventured to meddle with things that he ought not, and with the most important and dangerous subjects.' He added that Galileo's book had been printed by a ruse. As to the objections to the book 'Galileo knows well enough what the objections are . . . because we have talked to him about them, and he has heard them all from us.' The Pope had acted, he said 'with the greatest consideration for Galileo,' and added that his own conduct towards Galileo had been far better than Galileo's to him, for Galileo had deceived him. The Pope was firmly convinced that religion had been imperiled.

The special commission reported after about a month that Galileo has transgressed orders in deviating from hypothetical treatment of the Copernican opinion and by decidedly maintaining it he has erroneously ascribed the phenomena of the tides to the stability of the sun and the motion of the earth, which do not exist; he has been deceitfully silent about the command laid upon him by the Holy Office in 1616, to relinquish the Copernican doctrine 'nor henceforth to hold, teach or defend it in any way whatsoever, verbally or in writing, etc.,' 'which injunction Galileo acquiesced in and promised to obey.' Furthermore, Galileo printed the *imprimatur* of Rome on the title page of the *Dialogues* without authority; he put the saving clause of the book in the mouth of a simpleton, etc. (A full account of this report is given in Gebler's 'Galileo,' English edition, pp. 172-3. It is only incidentally of importance to us here.)

On the fifteenth of September, 1632, the Pope notified Niccolini that Galileo's affair was to be transferred to the inquisition. This was astounding news to the ambassador, who had all along believed that no proceedings would be taken against the astronomer and that the very worst to be feared was perhaps a command to alter certain phrases of the book. In the interview the Pope said 'Galileo was still his friend'—but that the Copernican opinion had been condemned sixteen years previously. At a meeting of the Congregation of the Holy Office held on September 23, it was pronounced that Galileo had disobeyed the command of February 26, 1616, and had concealed the prohibition then received by him from the censor at the time he applied for the *imprimatur* for his book; the inquisitor at Florence was, on the same day, by command of the Pope, directed to summon Galileo to appear before the commissary-general of the Holy Office in

Room, 'as soon as possible, in the course of the month of October.' On October 1, Galileo, in writing, acknowledged the receipt of the summons and promised to present himself during October, as directed.

The correspondence of Galileo shows that the summons came as a complete surprise to him, and he could not have received it without grave apprehension. He had risked everything in the belief that the Pope's favor and friendship would continue; but it is plain that this order would never have been despatched unless that favor had been withdrawn; his enemies had triumphed; he was at the mercy of men who would show no mercy to him personally—as in times past he had shown no mercy to them; even his friends among the Roman notabilities were powerless in the face of the Pope's anger; and his most influential supporter—Prince Cesi—was dead. There can have been no moments in all of Galileo's long life so bitter as these. The whole fabric he had built up in his imagination crumbled in an instant. Numberless incidents that he had formerly interpreted in one way must have arisen in his mind demanding new and more veracious interpretations that could be reconciled with the present bewildering reversal of all his hopes and beliefs. The Holy Office would have no difficulty in proving him culpable of disobedience to its orders; the general prohibition binding on all catholics he had openly disobeyed, as well as the prohibitions special to his case.

A letter written on October 13 to one of the cardinals, Barberini, shows Galileo's consternation and astonishment. He curses the time, he says, devoted to his studies. He begs the cardinal to intercede with the wise fathers in Rome, not to release him from giving an account of himself, which he is ready and anxious to do—but to make it easiest for him to obey. He can give his account in two ways; he can write a full history of his whole connection with the Copernican controversy which will prove to any one free from party malice that he has all along acted piously and as a good catholic; or he can give it verbally to the officers of the Inquisition in Florence. If, however, no dispensation or delay can be granted he will make the journey to Rome in spite of his great age and many bodily infirmities. The Tuscan ambassador at Rome interested himself in the matter, and throughout the whole of Galileo's process was devoted, prudent, wise and unwearied. No son could have been more faithful, nor more delicate. The letter was delivered, but the Pope would not permit delay. Galileo must come to Rome to answer. Niccolini then appealed directly to the

Pope, begging for delay on account of Galileo's infirmities. The answer was that he must come—slowly, if necessary—with every comfort—but he must be tried in person, 'for having been so deluded as to involve himself in these difficulties, from which we had relieved him when we were cardinal.' On the ninth of December orders were sent to Florence to compel Galileo to set out. A medical certificate of the seventeenth by Galileo's physicians pronounced him unfit to travel. The certificate was not believed in Rome, and Niccolini reported on the thirtieth that it was intended to send a physician from Rome with a commissioner who would, if he were fit to travel, bring him to Rome in chains.

On January 11, 1633, the Grand Duke wrote to Galileo advising him to set out, offering him one of the Court litters to travel in, and the hospitality of the ambassador's palace in Rome. On the twentieth of January Galileo left Florence on his last journey to Rome, arriving there, after a tedious quarantine, on February 13. Galileo, though technically a prisoner, was permitted to reside at the ambassador's palace. He writes to the Tuscan secretary of state that his treatment indicates 'mild and kindly treatment very different from the threatening words, chains and dungeons.' He was allowed to drive out, the shades of the carriage being half-drawn. His letters show that he was full of hope. It was now more than four months since he had been cited to appear, and in this time he must have considered what form the charges were to take and what defense he should make. Niccolini's despatch of February 27, 1633, says:

> The main difficulty consists in this—that these gentlemen maintain that in 1616 he [Galileo] was ordered neither to discuss the question [the Copernican opinion] nor to converse about it. He says, on the contrary, that these were not the terms of the injunction which were that that doctrine was not to be held or defended. He considers that he has the means of justifying himself, because it does not at all appear from his book that he does hold or defend the doctrine nor that he regards it as a settled question, as he merely adduces the reasons, *hinc hinde*. The other points appear to be of less importance and easier to get over.

From this despatch of Galileo's friend it appears that his defense was settled upon. The certificate of Cardinal Bellarmine was to be submitted to his judges; and it was to be proved from his book that he had obeyed the orders of the cardinal. Nothing was left undone by Niccolini, Castelli, or by the Grand Duke, to forward Galileo's interests. The Duke wrote letters of recommendation to the ten cardinals who made up the Holy Office, and some of the cardinals read the *Dialogues* and discussed them with Castelli. On April 12 Galileo was cited to appear at the Palace of the Inquisition. He acknowledged the *Dialogues* to be his own work. He was then asked to recount the proceedings of 1616 and replied that Cardinal Bellarmine had then told him 'that the aforesaid opinion of Copernicus might be held as a conjecture, as it had been held by Copernicus, and his eminence was aware that, like Copernicus, I only held that opinion as a conjecture,' which is evident from a letter (dated April 12, 1615) from the cardinal to Foscarini, in which he says: "It appears to me that your Reverence and Signor Galileo act wisely in contenting yourselves with speaking *ex suppositione* and not with certainty."

"In the month of February, 1616, Signor Cardinal Bellarmine told me that as the opinion of Copernicus, if adopted absolutely, was contrary to Holy Scripture, it must neither be held or defended, but that it might be held hypothetically and written about in this sense." Here Galileo presented a copy of the certificate which declares that the doctrine of Copernicus 'is contrary to the Holy Scriptures and therefore cannot be defended or held.' The Inquisition then asked if any other command was communicated to him and if he would remember it, if what was then said was read aloud to him. Galileo replied: "I do not remember that anything else was said or enjoined upon me, nor do I know that I should remember what was said to me, even if it were read to me. I say freely what I do remember, because I do not think that I have in any way disobeyed the injunction, that is, have not by any means held or defended the said opinion that the earth moves and the sun is stationary." The Inquisition now remind Galileo that a command was issued to him, before witnesses, enjoining "that he must neither hold, defend nor teach that opinion in any way whatsoever.' The annotation commands Galileo to 'relinquish altogether' the Copernican opinion, and forbids him 'henceforth to hold, teach or defend it in any way whatsoever, verbally or in writing; otherwise proceedings would be taken against him in the Holy Office; which injunction the said Galileo acquiesced in and promised to obey."

The Inquisition asks if Galileo remembers how and by whom the words first quoted were intimated to him. He replies: "I do not remember that the command was intimated to me by anybody but by the cardinal verbally; and I remember that the command was 'not to hold or defend.' It may be that 'and not to teach' was also there. I do not remember it, neither the definition 'in any way whatsoever,' but it may be that it was, for I thought no more about it, nor took any pains to impress the words on my memory, as a few months later I received the certificate now produced of the said Signor Cardinal Bellarmine, of twenty-sixth May, in which the injunction 'not to hold or defend' that opinion is expressly to be found. The two other definitions of the said injunction that have just been made known to me, namely, 'not to teach,' and 'in any way,' I have not retained in my memory, I suppose, because they are not mentioned in the said certificate on which I rely and which I have kept as a reminder."

Emphasis is laid by Gebler in his *Galileo* on the difference between an injunction 'not to teach' and one 'not to hold or defend.' I can see no essential difference between forbidding a citizen of Russia, let us say, from holding or defending anarchistic opinions and forbidding him from holding, teaching or defending such opinions in any way whatsoever, verbally or in writing. The latter prohibition is more formal. It is not more absolute. The annotation of February 26, 1616, is received throughout the process by the Inquisitors as exact in all particulars. *It is not denied by Galileo*; he says merely that he does not recall certain parts of it. It does not formally appear that the witnesses to it were called to testify. If they had been called their recorded testimony would have settled certain points that must now be settled from the text of the annotation itself. I can see no reason to doubt that the words of the text mean precisely what they say.

This is perhaps the place to say that the documents of Galileo's process have been examined again and again and that each examination has proved that the papers have not been tampered with in any manner and that they represent the case as it was understood by the Holy Office with minute accuracy. The hearing for the first day was closed with further questions and answers. Galileo was asked whether after the aforesaid command was issued to him he received permission to write the *Dialogues*. He replied: "After receiving the command aforesaid I did not ask permission to write the book . . . because I did not consider that in writing it I was acting contrary to, far less disobeying, the command not to hold, defend, or teach, the said opinion." The next questions relate to the printing of the book and Galileo is asked if he had informed the censor of the command aforesaid. He replies: "I did not say anything about the command to the master of the palace . . . for I have neither maintained nor defended the opinion that the earth moves and the sun is stationary in that book, but have rather demonstrated the opposite of the Copernican opinion and shown that the arguments of Copernicus are weak and not conclusive." Galileo's defense is here outlined. It is to be that he did not 'hold' the Copernican opinion after 1616. Not holding it, he did not defend it, nor teach it. Hence he had disobeyed no command, he maintains, although it is obvious to all that the *Dialogues*, like his other writings, are a brilliant defense of the system of Copernicus.

An apartment of 'three large and comfortable rooms' was assigned to Galileo in the Palace of the Holy Office, as he was their prisoner. His servants stayed with him. His meals were sent in by the devoted Niccolini, to whom he wrote every day with perfect freedom. His own account of the proceedings of the first day of his examination is as follows:

> I arrived in Rome on the tenth of February and I was placed in the clement charge of the Inquisition and of the Sovereign pontiff, Urban VIII., who esteemed me although I could not rhyme epigrams and little love-sonnets. I was placed in arrest in the delicious palace of . . . the Ambassador of Tuscany. The next day I received the visit of P. Lancio, Commissary of the Holy Office, who took me with him in his carriage. On the way he questioned me, showing a great desire that I should repair the scandal I had raised throughout all Italy by maintaining the opinion of the motion of the earth. To all the mathematical reasons that I could bring forward he answered one thing only. *Terra autem in æternum stabit, quia terra in æternum stat*, as the Scripture saith.

Thus discoursing, we arrived at the palace of the Holy Office. I was presented, by the commissary, to the assessor with whom I found two Dominican monks. They notified me, with civility, that I should be permitted to explain my reasons to the congregation, and that, subsequently, my excuses would be heard if I were judged culpable. The following Sunday I appeared, in fact, before the congregation and proceeded to set forth my proofs. To my ill-fortune they were not satisfying; no matter what pains I took I could not succeed in making myself understood. My arguments were interrupted by their zeal, they spoke only of the scandal I had caused, always bringing up the passage of Scripture referring to the miracle of Joshua, as the unanswerable portion of the matter. This reminded me of another passage in which the language of the Bible is entirely conformable to popular notions—(The heavens are solid and polished like a mirror of brass). This example seemed to me to be opposite to prove that the words of Joshua could be so interpreted and the conclusion seemed to me to be entirely just. But they gave it no weight and I was answered only by shrugging of shoulders.

Galileo's own account of the proceedings gives a different impression from that of the official record. He was argumentative about texts of Scripture, and when his explanation of Joshua's miracle was not found satisfactory, he suddenly recalls another text which will convince the Inquisitors, he thinks, that

Scripture is not to be interpreted literally. They answered by shrugging their shoulders and by again referring to the scandal he has created in the Church. Galileo does not seem to have, even yet, realized the situation. A letter from the commissary-general of the Inquisition to Cardinal Francesco Barberini (dated April 28, 1633) explains the events of the next weeks. The letter states that the commissary has informed the cardinals of the Holy Office regarding Galileo's case, and that they "took into consideration various difficulties with regard to the manner of pursuing the case and of bringing it to an end. More especially as Galileo has in his examination denied what is plainly evident from the book written by him; since in consequence of this denial there would result the necessity for greater rigor of procedure and less regard to other considerations belonging to this business. Finally I suggested a course, namely, that the Holy Congregation should grant me permission to treat extra-judicially with Galileo, in order to render him sensible of his error, and to bring him, if he recognizes it, to a confession of the same . . . permission was granted me. That no time might be lost, I entered into discourse with Galileo yesterday afternoon, and after many arguments and rejoinders had passed between us, by God's grace I attained my object, for I brought him into a full sense of his error. . . . The affair is being brought to such a point that it may soon be settled without difficulty. The court will maintain its reputation; it will be possible to deal leniently with the culprit. . . ."

Who can say what the arguments of the commissary of the inquisitor were? They were effective. Galileo's attitude was utterly and instantly changed. On the thirtieth of April he again appeared before the Holy Office and read the following confession:

In the course of some days continuous and attentive reflection . . . it occurred to me to reperuse my printed dialogue, which for three years I had not seen, in order carefully to note whether, contrary to my most sincere intention, there had, by inadvertence, fallen from my pen anything from which a reader or the authorities might infer not only some taint of disobedience on my part but also . . . that I had contravened the orders of the Holy Church. . . . I freely confess that in several places it seemed to me set forth in such a form that a reader ignorant of my real purpose might have had reason to suppose that the arguments adduced on the false side, which it was my intention to confute, were so expressed as to be calculated rather to compel conviction by their cogency than to be easy of solution.

Two arguments there are in particular—one taken from the solar spots, the other from the ebb and flow of the tide—which in truth, come to the ear of the reader with far greater show of force and power than ought to have been imparted to them by one who regarded them as inconclusive, and who intended to refute them, as I truly and sincerely held and do hold them to be inconclusive and admitting of refutation.

And, as excuse to myself for having fallen into an error so foreign to my intention, not contenting myself entirely with saying that when a man recites the arguments of the opposite side with the object of refuting them, he should, especially if writing in the form of dialogue, state these in their strictest form, and should not cloak them to the disadvantage of his opponents—not contenting myself, I say, with this excuse—I resorted to that of the natural complacency which every man feels with regard to his own subtleties and in showing himself more skilful than the generality of men, in devising them, even in favor of false propositions, ingenious and plausible arguments. With all this, although with Cicero's *'avidior gloriæ quam satis est'* if I had now to set forth the same reasonings, without doubt I should so weaken them that they should not be able to make an apparent show of that force of which they are really and essentially devoid. My error, then, has been—and I confess it—one of vainglorious ambition, and of pure ignorance and inadvertence.

This is what it occurs to me to say with reference to this particular, and which suggested itself to me during the reperusal of my book.

This confused and almost incoherent confession is totally unlike the precise and elegant phrases of Galileo's writings. It is a complete reversal of his former position. Parts of it are evidently mere reminiscences of his conversation with the commissary-general ('vainglorious ambition,' for instance, is a phrase that he must have accepted, not one originating with himself). The whole is a weak abandonment of a position proudly held and is as different as possible from the manly attitude of Cremonini—an attitude, be it remarked, which he successfully maintained in the face of the Inquisitors. No one can read it without pity. It can be interpreted in many differing ways. My own interpretation is that Galileo was persuaded to make the confession by representations that the case was very serious indeed and that a general admission of the sort would satisfy the Pope and cardinals; and that after the confession was obtained it was not very difficult for his judges to proceed to the abjuration; while if the abjuration had been first proposed Galileo might have desperately refused to make it, thus precipitating a crisis most unwelcome to the Holy Office. This is mere conjecture and is perhaps not worth recording. Certain it is that, the confession once extorted, all the dignity of Galileo's attitude was lost. By a slight increase of pressure one who had already yielded so much could be made to yield more, and finally to yield all. It seems to be clear that the pressure was gradually applied.

The confession was received by the congregation. Galileo withdrew; but almost immediately returned to offer to write a continuation of his *Dialogues* which should most effectually confute the arguments of the earlier portions. This offer is interpreted by Gebler as 'weakness and insincere obsequiousness.' It appears to me to be simply an attempt on his part to prevent the condemnation and prohibition of his book; and to show that he was, even yet, far from realizing the grimness of the situation. Immediately after the hearing, Galileo, still a prisoner of the Inquisition, was permitted to return to the palace of the Tuscan ambassador. He wrote letters (which are not extant) to friends. Their answers show that he 'entertained the most confident hopes of a successful and speedy termination of his trial.' One of them writes (May 12) from Florence: "I have for a long time had no such consolatory news as that which your letter of the seventh brought me. It gives me well-founded hopes that the calumnies and snares of your enemies will be in vain . . . since you have gained far more than you have lost by the calamity that has fallen upon you. My pleasure is still more enhanced by the news that you expect to be able to report the end of the affair in your next letter."

On May 10, Galileo was again summoned and was informed that eight days would be allowed him to prepare a defense. He, however, had already prepared it and at once submitted the following:

When asked if I had signified to the R. P. the Master of the Palace the injunction privately laid upon me, about sixteen years ago, by orders of the Holy Office, not to hold, defend or 'in any way' teach the doctrine of the motion of the earth and the stability of the sun, I answered that I had not done so. And not being questioned as to the reason why I had not intimated it, I had no opportunity to add anything further. It now appears to me to be necessary to state the reason in order to demonstrate the purity of my intention, ever foreign to the employment of simulation or deceit in any operation I may engage in. I say, then, that as at that time reports were spread abroad by evil-disposed persons, to the effect that I had been summoned by the Lord Cardinal Bellarmine to abjure certain of my opinions and doctrines, and that I had consented to abjure them, and also to submit to punishment for them, I was thus constrained to apply to his Eminence, and to solicit him to furnish me with a certificate, explaining the cause for which I had been summoned before him; which certificate I obtained, in his own handwriting and it is the same that I now produce with the present document.

From this it clearly appears that it was merely announced to me that the doctrine attributed to

Copernicus of the motion of the earth and the stability of the sun must not be held or defended and (here the original MS. is defaced) . . . beyond this general announcement affecting every one, any other injunction in particular was intimated to me, no trace thereof appears there. Having, then, as a reminder, this authentic certificate in the handwriting of the very person who intimated the command to me, I made no further application of thought or memory with regard to the words employed in announcing to me the said order not to hold or defend the doctrine in question; so that the two articles of the order—in addition to the injunction not to 'hold' or 'defend' it—to wit the words 'nor to teach it' 'in any way whatsoever—which I heard are contained in the order intimated to me, and registered—struck me as quite novel and as if I had not heard them before; and I do not think I ought to be disbelieved when I urge that in the course of fourteen or sixteen years I had lost all recollection of them . . . whence it appears to me that I have a reasonable excuse for not having notified to the Master of the Sacred Palace the command privately imposed upon me ..." [then follows a paragraph declaring that the faults scattered through this book 'have not been artfully introduced' but are inadvertent, owing to a vainglorious ambition and complacency . . . which fault he is ready to correct.]

Lastly, it remains for me to pray you to take into consideration my pitiable state of bodily indisposition to which, at the age of seventy years, I have been reduced by ten months of constant mental anxiety . . . ; [and he hopes that his judges may remit (his punishment) and may defend his honor and reputation against the calumnies of ill-wishers].

No one can read this confession and defence without a feeling of deep pity. This is even intensified if we find in it a lack of entire candor as it is hard not to do—'mistrust in the truthfulness of the accused'—is Gebler's phrase. Galileo returned to his palace feeling that his confession had served him well and that his trial was to come to a favorable issue. His confession had, however, put him in the power of his judges. They believed that now was the time to make a signal example. It was decided by the congregation (June, 1633) to bring Galileo to trial 'as to his intention and under threat of torture.'

On the morning of June 21 Galileo appeared before the Holy Office, and after being sworn was questioned. His first answer was:

A long time ago, that is before the decision of the Holy Congregation of the Index . . . I was indifferent and regarded both opinions, namely that of Ptolemy and that of Copernicus, as open to discussion, inasmuch as either one might be true to nature; but after the said decision, assured of the wisdom of the authorities, I ceased to have any doubt; and I held and still hold, as most true and indisputable, the opinion of Ptolemy, that is to say, the stability of the earth and the motion of the sun.

Questioned upon the publication of his *Dialogues*, he answers in accordance with his previous utterances. 'I am here to obey,' he says, 'and I have not held this opinion since the decision was pronounced.' The protocol of his trial concludes with the words: (Galileo's) 'signature was obtained to his deposition and he was sent back to his place.' This place was not the palace of the Tuscan ambassador. Galileo was detained at the building of the Holy Office till June 24. It is the opinion of the best judges that Galileo was not confined in the dungeons of the Inquisition.

There is not in the Vatican manuscript of the protocol, or in any other place, any evidence or any hint that Galileo was put to the torture at this or at any time. That he was threatened with the torture is equally certain. If he had boldly professed the Copernican opinion the proceedings would have taken a course that had been prescribed in advance (June 16). As he was disposed to abjure this opinion the course was different.

On the twenty-second of June, 1633, Galileo was brought into the presence of his judges, where his sentence was pronounced. The sentence of Galileo is a long document. The following extracts contain the points of especial importance.

We the undersigned (the names are given), by the Mercy of God, Cardinals of the Holy Roman Church, Inquisitors-general throughout all the Christian Republic, deputed by the Holy Seat against heretical perversity:

Whereas, you, Galileo, son of the late Vincenzio Galilei, Florentine, aged 70 years, *were denounced, in 1615, to this Holy Office, for holding as true a false doctrine* proposed by several authors, *that is to say, that the sun is immovable . . .* ; and moreover for having had certain disciples to whom you taught the same doctrine; for having corresponded on this subject with certain mathematicians of Germany; for having made public certain letters on the subject of spots upon the Sun in which you expounded the said doctrine as true; and whereas you answered, when objections were made to you citing to you passages of Scripture, by explaining the said Scripture in your own manner; and whereas a copy of a letter was shown to you, said to have been written by you to one of your former disciples (Castelli), in which you, still maintaining the hypotheses of Copernicus, interpreted several propositions contrary to the meaning and the authority of Holy Writ:

This Holy Tribunal being therefore desirous of proceeding against the disorder and mischief thence resulting . . . the two propositions of the stability of the Sun and the motion of the earth were . . . qualified as follows:

The proposition that the sun is the center of the world and does not move from its place is absurd and false philosophically, and formally heretical, because it is expressly contrary to the Holy Scripture.

The proposition that the earth is not the center of the world and immovable, but that it moves, and also with a diurnal motion, is equally absurd and false philosophically, and theologically considered, at least erroneous in faith.

But whereas *at the same time* it was our pleasure to proceed against you with benignity, *it was decided in the Holy Congregation . . . February 25, 1616, that the Very Eminent Cardinal Bellarmine should enjoin you to quit entirely the said false doctrine, not to teach it to others, not to defend it, never to treat it, under penalty that, if you failed to agree to this precept you would be thrown into a prison*, and for the execution of this decree, on the following day, in the Palace, in presence of the said Cardinal Bellarmine, after having been benignly admonished by him, *you received* from the Commissary of the Holy Office, *in the presence of* a notary and of *witnesses the injunction to desist entirely from the said opinion and for the future it was* forbidden to you to defend it, or to teach it in any way, whether by word of *mouth or by writing; and having promised obedience, you were dismissed . . .* and, *whereas, there appeared last year, at Florence, a book whose title named you as the author . . . in which was found a manifest transgression of the aforesaid ordinance intimated to you, and as in that book you defended the opinion that had been condemned*, although, in the book, by various devices, you endeavored to persuade that you left that opinion undecided and expressly probable, which is in itself a very grave error, since an opinion cannot be probable when it has been declared and defined to be contrary to Holy Writ:

It is for this reason that, by our order, you have been *called to this Holy Office, where, examined upon oath, you, admitted that the said book was written and published by you; you confessed that it was commenced about twelve years ago*, after having received the injunction above-named, *and that you asked permission to publish it without signifying* to those who were empowered to grant permission, *that you had been enjoined from holding, defending or teaching such doctrine in any manner whatsoever.*

You also confessed that the said book in several places is so written that the arguments in favor of a false opinion may appear to be of a nature to force agreement, rather than such as to be easily refutable; *you excused yourself for falling into an error foreign to your intention* on account of the dialogue form and because of one's natural inclination to show oneself more acute and more subtle than the generality of men. . . .

And whereas delay had been granted you to prepare your defense you produced a letter from Cardinal Bellarmine, that you had obtained from him in order to defend yourself from the calumnies of your enemies who had spread abroad that you had abjured and that you had been punished by the Holy Office. This letter declares that you did not abjure nor were you punished; that you had only been notified of the declaration . . .

that the doctrine of the motion of the earth . . . is contrary to the Holy Scriptures and that it cannot be held or defended; and that as no mention was made in it of the prohibition of teaching in any manner whatever, it is to be believed that in the course of fourteen or sixteen years, this especial thing escaped your memory, and that this is the reason you said nothing of it when asking permission to print, and that in so speaking, you do not wish to excuse your error which should be imputed to a vainglorious ambition rather than to ill intention. But even this certificate, produced in your defense, only makes your cause worse, since it is there said that the said opinion is contrary to Holy Writ, and nevertheless you have dared to treat and defend it, etc., and *the permission* (to print) *that you obtained by ruse cannot help you.* . . .

And as it appeared to us that you did not speak the whole truth concerning your intentions, we judged it necessary to proceed to a rigorous examination at which . . . you answered like a good Catholic. . . . Therefore, having considered the merits of your case, with your confessions and excuses, and all that ought justly to be seen and considered, we have arrived at the underwritten final sentence against you . . . we say that *you*, the said *Galileo . . . have rendered yourself* . . . vehemently *suspect of heresy* . . . and that consequently you have incurred all the censures and penalties imposed . . . against such delinquents. From which *we are content that you be absolved, provided that first . . . you abjure,* curse and detest the aforesaid errors (and) heresies . . . in the form to be prescribed by us, . . . and we ordain that the book of the *Dialogues* . . . be prohibited by public edict.

We condemn you to the formal prison of this Holy Office during our pleasure, and by way of salutary penance, we enjoin that for three years you repeat the seven penitential psalms once weekly, reserving to ourselves full liberty to moderate . . . the aforesaid penalties . . . [signatures of seven cardinals—three not being present or not signing.]

The abjuration of Galileo is the last document of the pitiable history:

I, Galileo Galilei, . . . aged seventy years, arraigned personally before this tribunal and kneeling before you . . . swear that I have always believed, do now believe and by God's help will for the future believe, all that is . . . taught by the Holy Catholic and Apostolic Roman Church. But whereas—*after an injunction* had been judicially intimated to me . . . *that I must altogether abandon the false opinion* that the sun is the center of the world and immovable, and that the earth is not the center of the world, and moves, and *that I must not hold, defend or teach in any way* whatever, verbally or in writing, *the said doctrine* and *after* it had been notified to me that *the said doctrine was contrary to Holy Writ— I wrote* and printed *a book in which I . . . adduce arguments* of great cogency in its favor . . . and for this cause I have been pronounced by the Holy Office to be vehemently suspected of heresy . . . *therefore desiring to remove . . . this strong suspicion*, reasonably conceived against me, with sincere heart and unfeigned faith *I abjure*, curse, and detest the aforesaid errors and heresies . . . and I swear that in future I will never again say or assert verbally or in writing, anything that might furnish occasion for a similar suspicion regarding myself; but that should I known any heretic . . . I will denounce him. . . . I the said Galileo have abjured, sworn, promised and bound myself as above . . . this twenty-second day of June, 1633.

Of the foregoing documents it is necessary to say that most have been translated from the French of Delambre, as the English translations of Gebler were not accessible at the time of writing. It is believed that the extracts given accurately represent the originals. Certain phrases have been printed in italics to emphasize the essential facts of the story.

It is also necessary to inquire whether the documents, as printed, correctly state the facts of the trial of Galileo, his explanations, confessions and abjurations. It was certainly within the power of the writers of them to state these facts falsely, or to place them in a false light. Everyone has to make up his mind for himself whether the foregoing documents are to be taken as correct statements of the circumstances before and during the trial, or not. It is assumed in this paper that they are, in this respect, correct.

It seems impossible to make anything more than a verbal distinction between an injunction 'not to teach' and one 'not to hold or defend.' An opinion that is held and defended to others is an opinion taught to them.

The words of Galileo's judges appear to mean precisely what they say. There was no need to distort them, for his confession of April 30 placed him completely at the mercy of his judges.

A discussion by Gebler (pp. 234-239) of the legality of the proceedings against Galileo and of the effect of the sentence against him brings out with complete demonstration the propositions that: 'the sentence of Galileo rests again and again, even on the principles of the ecclesiastical court itself, on an illegal foundation'; that 'Roman Catholic posterity can say to this day'—with truth—"that Paul V. and Urban VIII. were in error 'as men' about the Copernican system, but not 'as Popes' "; and that "the conditions which would have made the decree of the congregation, or the sentence against Galileo, of dogmatic importance were wholly wanting. Both Popes had been too cautious to endanger (the) highest privilege of the papacy, by involving their infallible authority in the decision of a scientific controversy."

There can be no doubt of the validity of these conclusions. The purpose of the prosecution was to check the spread of Copernican doctrines among the faithful and to utterly ruin the authority of Galileo. This purpose was fully attained when notice of his abjuration and punishment was sent to all vicars "so that it may come to the knowledge of all professors of philosophy and mathematics . . . that they may understand the gravity of the fault he has committed as well as the punishment they will have to undergo should they (likewise) fall into it." (July 2, 1633).

There is no need to trace the further history of Galileo's life in detail. He was permitted to return to the neighborhood of Florence and there he lived until his death in 1642—the year of Newton's birth.

His friend and pupil Castelli writes of his death:

The noblest eye which nature ever made is darkened; an eye so privileged, and gifted with such rare powers that it may truly be said to have seen more than the eyes of all that are gone, and to have opened the eyes of all that are to come.

The year 1638 was marked by the publication of his epoch-making book 'Discourses on two new Sciences appertaining to Mechanics and Motion.' This contained the foundation of the modern doctrine of mechanics and it is the crowning glory of Galileo's life. It attracted instant and universal attention, and at the age of seventy-four Galileo was again recognized by all Europe as a master of science—a founder of doctrine. The troubles of his later years grew light in the satisfaction of his legitimate pride.

Myths have grown up about the history of Galileo that it is not necessary to destroy. The whole distressing story has been told in authentic documents. He never suffered bodily torture; he was humiliated and discredited. He never even dared to whisper: *E pur se muove*. His history, though misinterpreted, has been of the deepest service to the world. It affords a symbol around which the rights of men to freedom of thought have clustered. Just as Benedict Arnold serves as the type of a traitor, so Galileo has been made to serve as a martyr of science. But he was no martyr. A true martyr does not abjure his opinions even in presence of the rack. While his recantation may be excused, it does not testify to moral greatness. We may add a paragraph from Gebler:

Party interests and passions have to a great extent and with few exceptions, guided the pens of those who have written on Galileo's life. The one side has lauded him as an admirable martyr of science, and ascribed more cruelty to the Inquisition than it really inflicted on him;

the other has thought proper to enter the lists as defender of the Inquisition, and to wash it white at Galileo's expense. Historic truth contradicts both.

Galileo was a genius of the first order. His title to lasting fame rests principally on his investigations in mechanics and physics, on the theory of the pendulum, the law of falling bodies, the invention of the thermometer, and on the intelligence with which he employed his unique opportunity for telescopic discoveries. His popular reputation will, however, always be based upon his re-invention of the telescope, his advocacy and proof of the Copernican system, his sufferings from the Inquisition, his torture, his abjuration, his seclusion at Arcetri. He will remain preeminently the martyr for science.

www.ingramcontent.com/pod-product-compliance
Lightning Source LLC
Chambersburg PA
CBHW031405040426
42444CB00005B/426